Some might say, for a pastor who b[...] the best job ever. I 100 percent agre[...] combined my faith in Jesus and call[...] passion for NFL football.

Del Duduit, in his third NFL devotional, does the same thing. With incredible real-life faith stories from NFL players, Del will challenge you to grow in your faith with thought-provoking questions, and he'll give you some practical steps for applying your faith to everyday life. If you love NFL football, and you want to grow in your faith in Jesus, you've picked up the right book.

—**Kent Chevalier**, Chaplain, Pittsburgh Steelers

Goal Line Devotions is another touchdown when it comes to devotional books from Del Duduit. This little gem puts you in the locker room with some of the biggest names in the NFL and lets you see how they handle success and failure and who they rely on when life gets tough.

This book will inspire you to do better every day and will prepare you to make the big play when it's third and long. I appreciate the personal touch Del puts into each chapter and how he inspires with quotes and scripture.

—**Gary Kidwell**, Kentucky High School
Athletic Association Hall of Fame

This book gives the reader behind-the-scenes insight into what it takes to be a champion on and off the gridiron. Through personal testimonies and unique illustrations that Del uses in this book, he makes each chapter applicable to the reader, which supplies this book with power to change a life. The truth, facts, and stories in *Goal Line Devotions* give the reader what it means to take the field for faith each day. Exceptional and inspirational.

—**Brendon Miller**, Bluegrass Sports Nation

In this book, *Goal Line Devotions*, Del takes you into the lives of some of the most recognizable names in the NFL and allows you to see how they have dealt with challenges and how God's love helped them through. He lets you see who the players credit for all they have in life and how they worship God no matter what happens—good or bad. Bravo, Del, on another great book.

—**Kevin Lewis**, Sportswriter, Lewis County Herald

More from Del Duduit

Stars of the Faith Series
Dugout Devotions
First Down Devotions
Dugout Devotions II
First Down Devotions II
Birdies, Bogeys & Blessings

Sports Shorts
Alabama Devotions
Auburn Devotions
Florida Devotions
Florida State Devotions

STARS OF THE FAITH

DEL DUDUIT

GOAL LINE
DEVOTIONS

Stories of Faith

from NFL's Best

IRON STREAM

Birmingham, Alabama

Goal Line Devotions

Iron Stream
An imprint of Iron Stream Media
100 Missionary Ridge
Birmingham, AL 35242
IronStreamMedia.com

Copyright © 2024 by Del Duduit

No part of this publication may be reproduced, stored in a retrieval system, or transmitted in any form or by any means—electronic, mechanical, photocopying, recording, or otherwise—without the prior written permission of the publisher.

Iron Stream Media serves its authors as they express their views, which may not express the views of the publisher. While all the stories in this book are true, some of the details and names have been changed or deleted to protect the storyteller's identity. All stories are used by permission.

Library of Congress Control Number: 2023944116

Scripture quotations unless otherwise marked are from the ESV® Bible (The Holy Bible, English Standard Version®), copyright © 2001 by Crossway, a publishing ministry of Good News Publishers. Used by permission. All rights reserved. The ESV text may not be quoted in any publication made available to the public by a Creative Commons license. The ESV may not be translated in whole or in part into any other language.

Scripture quotations marked KJV are from The Authorized (King James) Version. Rights in the Authorized Version in the United Kingdom are vested in the Crown. Reproduced by permission of the Crown's patentee, Cambridge University Press.
Scripture quotations marked NKJV are taken from the New King James Version®. Copyright © 1982 by Thomas Nelson. Used by permission. All rights reserved.
Scripture quotations marked (NLT) are taken from the Holy Bible, New Living Translation, copyright ©1996, 2004, 2015 by Tyndale House Foundation. Used by permission of Tyndale House Publishers, Carol Stream, Illinois 60188. All rights reserved.

Cover design by Jonathan Lewis / Jonlin Creative

ISBN: 978-1-56309-680-8 (paperback)
ISBN: 978-1-56309-681-5 (e-book)

1 2 3 4 5—28 27 26 25 24

This little book is dedicated to my grandson, Micah.

Although this was written and dedicated before you were born, I wanted to make sure it was meant for, and inspired by, you.

You have already overcome challenges, and I am confident, with God's grace and merciful plan, that you will be a wonderful blessing to me and your family.

You are precious in my sight as well as His.

CONTENTS

Foreword................................... xi
Acknowledgments........................... xiii
  1. Do Something About Your Praise.............. 1
    Evan McPherson

  2. What Is Your Identity?...................... 7
    Alex Highsmith

  3. Find Your Favor........................... 13
    Noah Brown

  4. You and God Can Go Together 19
    Chase Edmonds

  5. Where Does Your Journey Begin? 25
    Jalen Ramsey

  6. Where Would You Be?...................... 31
    Melvin Ingram

  7. Welcome Back 37
    Levi Wallace

  8. God Is Greater Than 43
    Logan Wilson

  9. God Loves You!........................... 49
    Jessie Bates III

10. What Is God Teaching You?................. 55
    Johnny Hekker

11. Be a Better Person 61
    Trey Hendrickson

12. Find Your Verse for Life 67
    Mike Hilton

13. Let Them See Jesus 73
    Diontae Johnson

14. Be the Man 79
    Chase Edmonds

15. When Peace Falls from the Car 85
    Cade York

16. God Is All You Need 91
    Trent Taylor

17. God's Love for You Is Amazing 97
    Tycen Anderson

18. Who Do You Play For? 103
    Jaylen Waddle

19. Think About the Positives 109
    Jalen Ramsey

20. God Will Provide a Safe Landing 115
    Jordan Kunaszyk

21. You Matter So Much to the Lord 121
    Hayden Hurst

22. Focus 127
    Corey Bojorquez

Contents

23. God Wants You on His Team 133
    Michael Thomas

24. Just Pray 139
    Tee Higgins

25. Make the Best Decision of Your Life 145
    Jordan Kunaszyk

26. You Are Never "Mr. Irrelevant" with God 151
    Brock Purdy

27. Make the Most of Your Second Chance 157
    Damar Hamlin

28. Don't Be Shy About Your Faith 163
    Patrick Mahomes

29. Be Who God Made You to Be 169
    Jalen Hurts

30. Know Your Purpose 175
    Cooper Kupp

FOREWORD

Ever since I was a kid, I loved watching NFL football. After Sunday service, I could not wait to get to my grandparents' house to scarf down some lunch just in time for kickoff. Growing up in Pittsburgh, I found there was nothing better than watching Terry Bradshaw, Franco Harris, and the Steel Curtain with my brother and cousins.

Now, as the Steelers team chaplain, I get to do something even better. Coach Mike Tomlin invited me to join the ministry of Athletes in Action, whose mission is to make disciples of Jesus in and through the NFL. I am privileged to come alongside these players and coaches to help them discover their faith, grow in their faith, and live out their faith.

For a pastor who bleeds black and gold, some might say that I have the best job ever. I 100 percent agree! I'm so grateful for the way God combined my faith in Jesus and calling of practical ministry with my passion for NFL football.

Del Duduit, in his third NFL devotional, does the same exact thing. With incredible real-life faith stories from NFL players, Del will challenge you to grow in your faith with thought-provoking questions, and he'll give you some practical steps for applying your faith to everyday life.

If you love NFL football, and you want to grow in your faith in Jesus, you've picked up the right book.

Here We Go!

Kent Chevalier
Pittsburgh Steelers Chaplain
Athletes in Action

ACKNOWLEDGMENTS

The following people played a big part in making this book come to life.

Thank you to:

My wife, Angie, for her support and love.

My agent, Cyle Young, for his faith in me and his love for the Bengals.

My publisher, John Herring, and all the gang at Iron Stream Media.

My editor, Susan Cornell, for her hard work to make this book better.

My colleagues at the *Portsmouth Daily Times*, Paul Boggs, Hope Comer, and Jacob Smith.

My Savior Jesus Christ for His love for me.

Chapter 1

DO SOMETHING ABOUT YOUR PRAISE

Evan McPherson
Placekicker

Therefore let us be grateful for receiving a kingdom that cannot be shaken, and thus let us offer to God acceptable worship, with reverence and awe.
—Hebrews 12:28

On the football field, Evan McPherson's confidence is evident when he boots a field goal or an extra point after a touchdown. Fans have become spoiled when he trots onto the turf because he usually nails it for points.

The Florida Gator product was drafted in the fifth round in the 2021 NFL Draft by the Cincinnati Bengals and had an immediate impact. He was the only kicker selected in the draft that year.

During the Bengals' 2021 playoff run, which included a Super Bowl appearance in Los Angeles, McPherson tied legendary kicker Adam Vinatieri for the most field goals made in a single postseason with fourteen. He also set the record for most postseason field goals made without a miss.

His clutch field goal kicking earned him the nickname "Money Mac" and the fifty-nine-yarder in the 2022 season established a franchise record.

His confidence is combined with humility and a grateful heart. But growing up, Evan was shy, especially when he attended church or any other function with others.

"I never really put my hands up in the air at church camp or church services, and I kept to myself a lot," he said. "I never really sang or praised God in front of a lot of people. It was just something I never did."

But the one thing that he recalls were the sermons from his pastor at youth camp. The Word of God found its way right into his heart.

"He was speaking directly to me, it seemed," Evan said. "He told us that Christians *should* worship God. That they should show appreciation for His blessings. After that, I just felt led to do something about it."

Evan started to lift his arms in praise to the Lord in church—and felt God's presence more and more. He liked it.

"I stuck my hands in the air and just worshipped my heart out," he added. "It was an amazing feeling."

He was challenged to come to the front and pray. After the prayer, a camp counselor took him aside and talked with him.

"I was bawling my eyes out, and I felt like I had a purpose," he said. "I wanted to live and strive to wake up every day and be a better person. When I worship, God makes me feel that way. I praise Him and He lifts me up. All my worries just go away when I praise God."

> *O Lord, you are my God;*
> *I will exalt you; I will praise your name,*
> *for you have done wonderful things,*
> *plans formed of old, faithful and sure.*
> —Isaiah 25:1

4th and Goal

How do you worship the Lord? Do you lift your arms in the air? Do you raise your hands up to honor Jesus Christ? Do you open your arms to accept His blessings and welcome them into your life? Do you shout or sing? There are many ways to glorify the Master for all He has done for you. Ask yourself this question: What do you do when your favorite kicker wins the game in overtime with a thirty-nine-yard field goal? Do you just sit there and acknowledge the victory? Do you just shrug it off or talk about the weather with your friends? Or do you scream and clap and jump up and down to celebrate? Perhaps you give your buddies high fives or pump your fists. Now let's revisit the original question. How do you worship the Lord?

Touchdown

You too might be shy like Evan was when he was younger. You might feel timid when you sit in church. Perhaps you don't want to bring attention to yourself. Or maybe the sanctuary you sit in is quiet or reserved. It doesn't matter what circumstances or environment you are in; God is worthy of your praise. If you don't praise the Lord, then the rocks will cry out in your place, according to Luke 19:40. There are many ways to glorify God. You can raise your arms and hands in worship. You may be led to run the aisles in a church service or demonstrate a holy dance. Some clap and others shout glory to God. When you praise the Lord, great things happen. Find your way to lift holy praises to the Lord. Here are some benefits to worship:

1. You will find a renewed strength. The Christian life can be a challenge, but it has the best rewards. The truth is, you cannot manage your life on your own. You need help and direction. Your humility and obedience will open the door for God's leadership. But when you praise Him, in good and bad times, your strength will be renewed, and you will find favor with the Lord. He will let you know that you will make it through. "Oh come, let us worship and bow down; let us kneel before the LORD, our Maker!" (Psalm 95:6).
2. You will be encouraged. Now more than ever, you need inspiration and motivation because today's world and culture is full of negativity and discouragement. Depression and anxiety are at an all-time high. When you stand and raise your arms to the Lord in praise, you will feel empowered and instant comfort. Your problems may not disappear, but you will have an encampment of angels to help you face the challenges. The world wants you to fail and will invite you to believe that you are not having fun and life is boring. However, serving God is the best life you can live. Praise God anyway. Find encouragement when you reach your arms to Him.

3. You will be set free. The chains of sin cannot hold you down when you praise the Lord and worship Him for what He has done. When you followed the devil and his advice, you were bound. The chains of discouragement held you down. God can set you FREE. Thank Him for that and praise Him for that. "For freedom Christ has set us free; stand firm therefore and do not submit again to a yoke of slavery" (Galatians 5:1).
4. Your faith will be stronger. Everyone goes through trials and struggles. You are not different. There might be times when doubt creeps into the huddle. And there might be times to trust His plan, especially when you find yourself down on the scoreboard. But when you can worship the Lord in times of struggle, your faith will also be lifted. When your favorite team or player is making a comeback, you have faith they will pull out the win. When you praise God, you focus on the good and great things He has done for you. God's goodness builds your faith.
5. You will be victorious. You are in a game of spiritual warfare. Sometimes you might feel that God is nowhere to be found. But it's just the opposite. He is waiting for you to stop focusing on the current situation and focus on His grace and mercy. Through praise, you can surrender your battle to God and let Him fight on your behalf. When He fights, He wins. And when He wins, you win. "What then shall we say to these things? If God is for us, who can be against us?" (Romans 8:31).

Evan learned early in life to praise the Lord. It brought him closer to God in his Christian journey. He surrendered all to Him. That doesn't mean he won't miss a field goal every now and then. It does mean that God will be with him in the huddle and will have his back no matter what challenges he faces. "Bad days will happen," he said. "In life and in football. But when I praise the Lord, I know everything will be OK."

Chapter 2

WHAT IS YOUR IDENTITY?

Alex Highsmith
Linebacker

Therefore if any man be in Christ, he is a new creature: old things are passed away; behold, all things are become new.
—2 Corinthians 5:17 KJV

On the gridiron, Alex Highsmith is a force to be reckoned with. He is feared by quarterbacks and running backs. Offensive linemen who try to block him are intimidated by his presence.

Fans and sportswriters alike noticed his dominance on defense. That's nothing new for Steeler Nation. For years, the black and gold faithful have had a defensive icon to admire. It was the Pittsburgh trademark.

Who will ever forget "Mean" Joe Greene, Jack Lambert, Troy Polamalu, Jack Ham or Rod Woodson—the legends of the Terrible Towels?

In week ten of the 2022 season, Alex had five tackles and forced a fumble to help lead the Pittsburgh Steelers to a 20–10 win over the New Orleans Saints. For his efforts, he was named the AFC Defensive Player of the Week. Many sportswriters in the Pittsburgh area labeled him as the team's MVP.

When the season was over, Alex posted sixty-three tackles and a team-high 14.5 sacks and led the NFL in forced fumbles with five. Alex is a true traditional professional football player. He loves to bring down quarterbacks and make the big stops on third downs more than anything. But that is what he does and not who he is. There is a big difference.

"My faith is the most important thing in my life," he said. "Whatever test God puts you through—trials or whatever—He really wants it to draw you closer to Him."

In 2018 at the University of North Carolina, Charlotte, Alex had a breakout season. He posted career-best performances in tackles, sacks, and tackles-for-losses. Alex also set the single-season school record with 17.5 tackles for losses and was named first team All-Conference USA. But he also sustained an injury that he had to lean on the Lord to overcome.

"During that time, I felt like there was a moment when God showed me more of Himself," he added. "I just felt like I needed to know that my identity was in Him and not on the field. I played football—but that's not who I was, and God was trying to show me that."

His mindset is simple. On his Twitter profile, he touts Luke 1:37 and believes that "nothing will be impossible with God."

"Some people might take that the wrong way," he said. "But at the end of the day, if it's His will, then God will bless you in so many ways. It's just a mindset that, when things go bad, He is able to turn it around if you just have the faith."

The faith he holds dear is what defines him now.

"Jesus died for me, and I've got to live for Him," he said. "That's why it's so important because all the things in this world are fleeting. I love this game of football, but it's not my god. I tried to put my identity in it at times in the past and it always let me down. I got hurt and couldn't make an impact. This game is great and I love it, but I'm not going to worship it. Having my foundation in Christ is what is important to me because He's always the same. Today, yesterday, and forever."

> *For we are his workmanship, created in Christ Jesus unto good works, which God hath before ordained that we should walk in them.*
>
> —Ephesians 2:10 KJV

4th and Goal

There is nothing wrong with success in the workplace. Alex enjoys that brand. He is a key player in the Steelers defense. He strives to be the best and is recognized for his efforts by the NFL, and he causes offensive coordinators to experience nightmares. If he does not give 100 percent or slacks off on plays, the coaches and fans will notice. In society, you might strive to get ahead in life and at work. Alex works hard off the field to play well on the field. Maybe you do the same in order to climb the corporate ladder. But is that who you are? How will you be remembered when you are no longer employed? At the end of the game, will your loved ones remember you for working late or for being there for them? Who are you? What defines you?

Touchdown

Do you live to work? Or do you work to live? You should always put in an honest day of work and expect an honest day of pay. There are some jobs that demand more of your time, but it should never dominate your identity. Alex is a professional football player, and he loves what he does. But he identifies as a Christian and a man of God. He does not back down from making a tackle or living his faith, and he enjoys using his platform to tell others about the love of Christ. Here are some ways you can be successful on the job—and a Super Bowl champion of a true believer of Christ.

1. Family first. This should always be your top priority. If your son has a part in the school play, but you have a report due to your manager the next day, prepare early for work and be there for your child. If your daughter is to be honored for her accomplishments, then be present. There are times when work must come first, but these should be few and far between.
2. Give your time. When you give your time and money to charity on a regular basis, you will put life in proper perspective. Find a cause that is important to you and become involved in some capacity. "And above all these things put on charity, which is the bond of perfectness" (Colossians 3:14 KJV).
3. Give back to God. You are commanded to give at least 10 percent of your income back to the Lord through your church. He gave you the job you hold. Don't be greedy or hoard your treasures. Jesus doesn't need your

money, but you need His blessings. "Honour the LORD with thy substance, and with the firstfruits of all thine increase" (Proverbs 3:9 KJV).

4. Help others in need. It doesn't take long to send a text or a card to a friend who is going through a tough time. People will remember you especially if you take the time to let them know you care. "Wherefore comfort yourselves together, and edify one another, even as also ye do" (1 Thessalonians 5:11 KJV).
5. Be a good ambassador for Christ. You don't have to be a preacher or a singer to minister. You can share your testimony in various ways. You are called to share the good news. Use your talents in ways to glorify the Lord. You can write a blog or share on social media. You don't need recognition for your efforts, but what you do for the Lord will not go unnoticed. Take food to nurses on the night shift at the hospital or visit families in hospice and pray with them.

You are a child of the King. Your main mission should be to find ways to identify as a Christian. Alex is a professional athlete, but that is not who he is as a person. You may wear many hats in life. Parent. Grandparent. Coach. Teacher. Pastor. CEO. Owner. Employee. Child of God. There are several titles you may earn, and some awards may even carry your name. That's great and should be commended, but is that who you want your loved one to remember you as? It's up to you. Your identity is waiting. Claim it through Christ.

Chapter 3

FIND YOUR FAVOR

Noah Brown
Wide Receiver

Why am I discouraged?
Why is my heart so sad?
I will put my hope in God!
I will praise him again—
my Savior and my God!
—Psalm 42:11 NLT

After being a part of the 2015 College Football Playoff National Championship team with The Ohio State Buckeyes, wide receiver Noah Brown had big hopes and plans. However, the Flanders, New Jersey, native did not anticipate lying in a hospital for two weeks prior to the next season.

Noah was having a strong spring practice with the Buckeyes and was in position to make the starting roster. Everything was going as planned. But he broke his left tibia during fall camp and had to redshirt the season and undergo two surgeries.

"There I was in a hospital bed for fourteen days instead of on the field with my teammates," Noah said. "To say I got discouraged was an understatement—I was really down. I had some doubts about my athletic future. I didn't know if I'd play again. But I knew I had to keep my faith and hold on to it, but it was hard. Really hard."

During that time, he was discouraged. He was only a few days away from starting as a sophomore with the defending national champions and excited and preparing for a great season when he was sidelined.

"I didn't count on that, by any means," he said. "You know there is always a risk, but you never really think it'll happen. It's in the back of your mind sometimes, but you think you're invincible too."

Noah worked hard during rehab and stayed focused on his goal and leaned on the Lord for strength and encouragement.

"I really think that time off built my character and made me focus on Him more and trust in my faith," he admitted. "My whole family is into faith and has faith, so it's something I grew up with. It was a big part of my growing up and is still the center of my life. I really fell back on my faith and it grew."

Noah came back in 2016 with the Buckeyes and claimed his role in the starting lineup. He started in all thirteen games and had thirty-two receptions for 402 yards with seven touchdowns. In the third week of the season against the University of Oklahoma, he tied a school record with four touchdowns and had five receptions for seventy-two yards.

After that season, he declared for the NFL Draft and was selected by the Dallas Cowboys in the seventh round.

He made it.

Noah came back from a serious injury to see his dreams of playing in the NFL a reality. Noah believed in Psalm 55:22, which says to "give your burdens to the LORD, and he will take care of you. He will not permit the godly to slip and fall" (NLT).

He sees that scripture every day because it's tattooed in an obvious spot.

"That's on my leg, right where I broke my leg in college and it's over that scar," he said. "I am a man of faith and that was intentional—any adversity can be met with Christ—that is what that's about. God is all over my scar because He brought me out of that."

The discouragement Noah went through for a short time was overtaken by faith. He trusted in the Word of God and saw his prayers answered.

Noah has another tattoo to let everyone know about how he feels about Jesus Christ. And it's personal. Genesis 6:8 reads "But Noah found favor with the LORD." That verse describes how Noah obeyed the Lord and built the ark.

"That verse was my first tattoo," he said. "That resonates with me. I am Noah, and I have found great favor with the Lord. It's just a reminder for me. I believe in the Lord Jesus Christ, and I know He loves me and keeps me in His favor."

> *The LORD keeps you from all harm*
> *and watches over your life.*
> *The LORD keeps watch over you as you come and go,*
> *both now and forever.*
> —Psalm 121:7–8 NLT

4th and Goal

Have you ever had your plans or hopes dashed by an unexpected event that was out of your control? How did you react? Did you allow the devil to blitz your mind and sack you when you were already down and discouraged? It happens. The enemy does not play fair and will take every opportunity to take you down. Maybe a job layoff blindsided you and your plans. Perhaps a medical test revealed some news you did not wish to hear. What do you lean on? Do you become angry, or do you snuggle up close with the Lord?

Touchdown

You can come back from a setback like Noah did in college. The time off he spent rehabbing his leg allowed his faith to become stronger. God got Noah's attention. His character also developed during that time. The same can happen to you. When struggles come, you can still find that wonderful relationship with Christ to help you through the dark times. Can you have favor with the Lord? Of course you can. Here are some ways to make sure you have God's favor.

1. Be cautious of praise from others. This can come to you in many forms. You might hold a position of power at work or on a board of directors. Those are wonderful, but you cannot let that influence you or puff you up. You are not any better than anyone else. "Obviously, I'm not trying to win the approval of people, but of God. If pleasing people were my goal, I would not be Christ's servant" (Galatians 1:10 NLT).

2. Be open to suggestions. Never have the attitude that your way is the only way to accomplish a goal. Being stubborn is not a desirable attribute. Be flexible to other ideas and suggestions, but never compromise your beliefs. "But those who exalt themselves will be humbled, and those who humble themselves will be exalted" (Matthew 23:12 NLT).
3. Never have an attitude of entitlement. You don't deserve anything—what you have achieved should be earned. When you think more of yourself and that you deserve certain "things," then you have a sense of entitlement. Instead, show gratitude and humility for what God has allowed you to enjoy. It could all be taken away in a snap. "Don't be selfish; don't try to impress others. Be humble, thinking of others as better than yourselves. Don't look out only for your own interests, but take an interest in others, too" (Philippians 2:3–4 NLT).
4. Do not put your faith in your own abilities. It's OK to have confidence in what you have learned and your talents, but always rely on God to use you for His glory. If you use it the wrong way, then you can also lose your talents. If you let them sit on the shelf, God could take them away. Whatever you do for the Lord, do it to the best of your ability.
5. Be aware of your weakness and never hide your struggles. You should know where you are vulnerable. That doesn't make you a weak person. In fact, it will allow you to grow. The devil knows your weakness, and so should you. When you inform others of your struggles, it will put you in a position to help others, which will

in turn strengthen you on your journey. "People who conceal their sins will not prosper, but if they confess and turn from them, they will receive mercy" (Proverbs 28:13 NLT).

To have favor with the Lord just means to be obedient. It means to be humble and thankful for what God has done for you. Noah found favor with Christ in his walk with the Lord. He knows that Jesus watches out for him and puts him in circumstances to help him grow. When you glorify the Lord for what He will do for you in advance, you will find God's favor.

Chapter 4

YOU AND GOD CAN GO TOGETHER

Chase Edmonds
Running Back

I can do all things through Christ who strengthens me.
—Philippians 4:13 NKJV

Some things just make a good fit and go together well. Like coffee and a sunrise. Snoopy and Woodstock. Milk and cookies. Macaroni and cheese. Batman and Robin. Scooby and Shaggy. Hammer and nails. Eggs and bacon. Well, bacon goes with everything, but you see the point.

It's not a surprise that Chase Edmonds's favorite verse is Philippians 4:13. The message is fabulous, and 4.13 is also his birthday.

"It just fits," Chase said. "I grew up on that passage of scripture too. I know I can do all things through Christ because He gives me strength."

Chase and Philippians 4:13—that's a good fit. His father told him that was a strong verse, and it's perfect for him. The verse inspires and motivates him.

"Any time I have doubts, or anytime I have battles, I go there," he said. "It's my go-to verse for sure. We all face battles and struggles every day and this verse helps me so much."

Chase was raised in a Christian home, and he knows that trials and tribulations are a part of life.

"I know I can hold on to the strength that God gives to me," he added. "I have that strength to get through, and I know my Father will get me through. I just try to stay in the Bible because it guides me. That's how I was raised. It's just my way of life."

The Fordham University All-American standout was drafted in the fourth round of the NFL Draft in 2018 by the Arizona Cardinals. He holds firm to his convictions and strives to be a positive role model to his teammates and fans.

"To me, being called a man of God means something," he said. "Anytime we have temptations—you know, like wrath, rage, jealousy, or whatever comes to trap you—you just think of God's promises to you and me. I want to live the way He wants me to live."

God's first commandment is the highest standard for Chase, and he knows that if he follows that lead, everything else in life falls into place.

In the twentieth chapter of Exodus, the first commandment tells us that there is no other god but Him.

"I just try to acknowledge that all the time," he said. "Whatever life gives me; I want to be known as a good man when I leave this earth and a man of God."

But it all begins with honoring and recognizing that first order that God is indeed God.

"That's where it all starts for me," he said. "If I didn't know that, then it's all fake. My God is first in my life. Then, that's where I know I can do all things through Him and through His strength."

For whatever things were written before were written for our learning, that we through the patience and comfort of the Scriptures might have hope.
—Romans 15:4 NKJV

4th and Goal

What does it mean to you to be a man of God? Or a person of God? Or a woman of God? What do you think it means? Will you be described that way? If not, it's never too late. There are many characteristics that could define this phrase. Maybe you have that desire to have that reference pointed at you. Some might describe you as hardworking, honest, charitable, kind. Or they might swing the other way and words you may not like could come out of people's lips. But there is still time to be placed into that wonderful description of being called a man or woman of God.

Touchdown

You might be a nice, sweet, and loving person, and that is good—to some point. Society has labeled a Christian as a person who is weak-minded and timid. The mainstream media and Hollywood sometimes portray a follower of Christ as a mindless alien aimlessly wandering through the world. But that's not who God wants you to be. What does it mean or take to be a person of God? Here are some suggestions to entertain.

1. Boldly proclaim your faith in Jesus Christ. This means you put the Lord first in everything you do. This includes your job, hobby, relationships, and your family. This does not mean to be a robot and constantly quote scripture. It means you live your life to honor the Lord. You don't go to places you know are wrong. You don't say words a Christian should not say. You allow the Lord to filter out the bad and insert the good. You are an instrument for His glory. "And in that day you will say: 'Praise the LORD, call upon His name; Declare His deeds among the peoples, Make mention that His name is exalted'" (Isaiah 12:4 NKJV).
2. Prioritize appropriately. God comes first. Family is next followed by your country and *then* your job. Some people may switch these around and place the occupation toward the top of the list. There are times when you cannot be at the House of God, but that should be infrequent. Be committed to going to church on a regular basis. Place the needs of your family in front of your own and never be ashamed of your country. The devil's main target of destruction is the family. Keep the target moving because it's hard to hit that way.
3. Develop a thick skin. Christians are targets of ridicule. Television programs portray followers of Christ like idiots and make fun of them all the time. This is

accepted by the secular world. You don't have to accept this, but you do have to deal with it because if you proclaim Christ, you will be attacked or ridiculed. The last thing you want to do is back down or demonstrate weakness when poked fun at. But it will happen. You must develop a way to handle it and be a good example of a Christian. "You have heard that it was said, 'An eye for an eye and a tooth for a tooth.' But I tell you not to resist an evil person. But whoever slaps you on your right cheek, turn the other to him also. If anyone wants to sue you and take away your tunic, let him have your cloak also" (Matthew 5:38–40 NKJV).

4. Establish solid friends. If you surround yourself with determined people of faith, then your strength will grow. People will hold you accountable and you can do the same. "As iron sharpens iron, so a man sharpens the countenance of his friend" (Proverbs 27:17 NKJV).

5. Give back. This can be done in several ways. Your time is valuable as well as your resources. You can volunteer in person or find an organization you believe in and support with your finances. "Give, and it will be given to you: good measure, pressed down, shaken together, and running over will be put into your bosom. For with the same measure that you use, it will be measured back to you" (Luke 6:38 NKJV).

Being considered a man or woman of God takes determination. You won't earn that stigma overnight. It's a long journey. If you make a mistake, learn from it and start over again. If Chase makes a mistake on the field, he brushes it off and gets ready for the next play. Be determined to run the race and be considered a person of God in the end. If it means taking responsibility for an action, then do that immediately. You cannot be fake and wear the honor of God. Make up your mind and be the person God wants you to be.

Chapter 5

WHERE DOES YOUR JOURNEY BEGIN?

Jalen Ramsey
All-Pro Cornerback

For I know the plans I have for you, declares the LORD, plans for welfare and not for evil, to give you a future and a hope.
—Jeremiah 29:11

Hope.

The word is defined by a feeling of expectation and desire for a certain thing to happen. It's also a feeling of trust. For example, during Super Bowl LVI, the Los Angeles Rams had hope in Jalen because of his defensive skills.

When this book was written, he was a three-time first-team All-Pro selection and a six-time Pro Bowl player. He is a college football national champion and a Super Bowl winner. His accolades and accomplishments speak for themselves.

That's one of many reasons the team he plays for has hope when Jalen takes the field. His presence is a sense of comfort.

But according to Jalen, his hope is 100 percent in the Lord Jesus Christ.

"It's all God," he said. "For me, growing up to play football, that's what He wanted for me, and He put me around the people and certain situations and gave me the ability. He let me stay in those situations, and he did not take me out of them. This is what He wanted for me. I'm grateful every day for His guidance."

Jalen's journey includes a Bowl Championship Series National Championship in college as a freshman in 2013 when he played for Florida State. He was the first true freshman to start for the Seminoles since "Prime Time" Deion Sanders in 1985. A few years later, in 2022, he was a key player for Los Angeles when the Rams defeated the Cincinnati Bengals in Super Bowl LVI. He truly believes this has been a part of God's plan for his life.

"He leads and He guides," Jalen said. "He lets you stay, or He takes you out. Obviously, He gives you free will to make choices and gives you opportunities to make decisions as long as you have a relationship with Him through Jesus Christ. You can hear His voice and you can listen to Him and, hopefully, you can follow His direction. He lights up my path and I follow—it's all God."

Jalen learns from the Word of God and from great men and women in the Bible. But he always goes back to one feature.

"I focus on my journey as a Christian," he said. "Everyone in the Bible has a different journey. Mine is unique to me, and I focus on mine. Some had purposes they were not able to fulfill, and some had hardships and had to seek forgiveness. They had to find and feel the grace of God. Nobody had the same journey and that is why I just focus on mine. I embrace my journey with the Lord. I learn from others, but this is *my* journey."

What gives the Smyrna, Tennessee, native hope?

"Reading the Word of God gives me hope," he said. "It gives me strength. I like to read through different stories and accounts because it helps me to look at mine. I always turn it to my journey because that's the one I'm living. Mine."

Everyone then who hears these words of mine and does them will be like a wise man who built his house on the rock.
—Matthew 7:24

4th and Goal

Are your personal goals in line with those of God's plan for you? How do you even know His plan for you? Maybe you went to college and obtained a diploma but have never found a job related to your degree. Or perhaps you have worked hard to achieve a goal only to run into obstacles and walls that prohibit you from reaching that destination. This can also be attributed to personal goals. Maybe the person you think you should date or marry does not feel the same way. God's redirection of your life can be frustrating, but it can also be a fun adventure.

Touchdown

Have you known a person who wants to sing, but God has not given them the talent? Ugh. That can be torture if you sit in the audience. Or maybe you want to play professional football, but you lack the physical stature needed to make the team. The question to figure out is, Are you wanting it, or does God want it for you? Trying to figure out what your plan is from the Lord can be frustrating, especially if you have no idea or don't want to go down that road. Waiting on His plan and timing can be irritating and confusing, especially if some around you are already on their path. Patience is something you must have. But here are some other things to consider when you want to find out what God wants you to do.

1. Surrender. This is easier said than done. But it must happen. Many times, when you say you are seeking God's will, you might be wanting Him to stamp an OK on your own selfish aspirations. Before the Lord will let you in on His plan, you must have an attitude of surrender. You must be ready to do anything He wants you to do—*anything*. "I appeal to you therefore, brothers, by the mercies of God, to present your bodies as a living sacrifice, holy and acceptable to God, which is your spiritual worship. Do not be conformed to this world, but be transformed by the renewal of your mind, that by testing you may discern what is the will of God, what is good and acceptable and perfect" (Romans 12:1–2).
2. Sacrifice. Consider a fast to draw closer to the Lord. Most of the time, this involves food. But a fast can also be something you like to do. For example, instead of going to your usual golf outing, spend that time in prayer. For a brief time, substitute a movie and read the Word of God and pray. Give up an activity or a

meal you enjoy and spend time with the Lord. He will notice and reward that if it's done with sincerity. "'Yet even now,' declares the LORD, 'return to me with all your heart, with fasting, with weeping, and with mourning'" (Joel 2:12).

3. Seek. You won't find it if you don't search. This goes for God's will. And it also applies to counsel from others. Take some time and consult with spiritual leaders who have experience. Listen to what they have to say and also be quiet and hear what God tells you through them. You have free will to make decisions, but choices that are made after consultation and prayer are wise ones.
4. Obey. If the Lord wants you to do something and you are hesitant, you need to give in and surrender to His will. It might be a test, or it may be the green light to go down a road you never thought of before. "For as by the one man's disobedience the many were made sinners, so by the one man's obedience the many will be made righteous" (Romans 5:19).
5. Trust. God wants what is best for you. You don't have to know the entire plan or the outcome. No one knows the future. People are put in your life for a reason, and you are placed in circumstances because of God's will—most of the time. You cannot expect the Lord to speak to you if you wander into a bar or a place you know you should not enter. Use common sense and talk to the Master and then do what He tells you. If you have kids, and they resist your rules, it may irritate or infuriate you because you know what's best for them. So does

Christ. "And we know that for those who love God all things work together for good, for those who are called according to his purpose" (Romans 8:28).

Everyone has different circumstances and personalities and dreams. God's plan for your life is important. For some, the plan is revealed early. For others, it may not be until midlife. No matter when or where, be ready when He puts you into the game and make the impact.

Chapter 6

WHERE WOULD YOU BE?

Melvin Ingram
Pro Bowl Linebacker

Oh give thanks to the Lord, for he is good; for his steadfast love endures forever!
—1 Chronicles 16:34

In the Super Bowl of life, you will face obstacles and many third-and-long situations. There will be moments when you must punt, and there will be situations where you come through in the clutch. Your determination and attitude play a big part in the outcome. If you doubt your arm strength and accuracy, then you may not find your receiver and turn the ball over on downs. But if you have prepared mentally, physically, and spiritually, you have a great opportunity to complete the pass and cross the goal line for a touchdown.

Melvin has that positive mentality all the time. He is aware of why he is on this earth and why he plays football at the highest level.

"None of us would be here without God," he said. "All the glory—and I mean ALL the glory goes to Him. We have to keep our faith no matter what happens. No matter what happens. Never get too high and never get too low. It's all about God and His plans for you."

In early 2013, Melvin tore his ACL and was expected to miss the entire season. This was not expected, and it allowed discouragement to creep into the huddle. But he worked hard in rehab and prayed and prayed and prayed. He never let those negative expectations bring him down and discourage him in those dark days.

"We all go through struggles and issues," he said. "In the way I was raised, God put His toughest soldiers through problems. We made it through, and He knew we'd make it through. You always have to give praise no matter what. If you trust and believe, then He will deliver you from those problems. It's just a matter of faith, perseverance, and patience. We all have problems, but God helps you get through those problems."

In week 16 of the season, Melvin was back on the field and sacked Raiders quarterback Matt McGloin and also forced a fumble. He collected his first postseason interception when he picked off Cincinnati Bengals quarterback Andy Dalton in the Wild Card round of the playoffs.

He was back before the experts anticipated.

"That happened the same way. I was determined, and I had God on my side," he added. "There is always a situation worse than yours. I just kept the faith. I stayed strong and kept pushing through and prayed. I knew things would be all right. Even at this level you go through a lot to get here. We are human, and we have problems. We have emotions and feelings. But I have the Lord on my side and that's what gets me through every day."

> *But by the grace of God I am what I am, and his grace toward me was not in vain. On the contrary, I worked harder than any of them, though it was not I, but the grace of God that is with me.*
>
> —1 Corinthians 15:10

4th and Goal

Life happens. You probably won't be in the starting lineup in the NFL, but stranger things can happen. But you might run into something like this in your life. The presentation you spent hours on for your manager was accidentally deleted by your child the day before it's due. Yikes! Or maybe you planned a trip for several weeks only to find out that the hotel is under construction when you arrive. Or maybe the person you have been courting suddenly wants to cool the relationship and just be friends. Those can invite discouragement and leave you in a frenzy of lousy moods. Life does not come with promises.

Touchdown

Attitude is an amazing thing. If it's bad, then it affects you in a negative way and influences everyone around you. If it's good, then you can inspire those in your circle and help you through each day. The more positive your attitude, the easier it will be for you to identify the silver lining in each challenge. And once you find that silver lining, you will possess the motivation to overcome negative issues. A positive attitude and a sense of gratitude are vital if you want to act and be successful. Here are some ways to have a grateful heart and a positive outlook.

1. Practice gratitude. Practice makes perfect. Be sure to count your blessings every day. You don't have to possess a large bank account or a new car to be happy. You don't have to be 100 percent healthy or out of debt to have peace in your heart. When you are grateful for what you have and your current situation, you can maintain a positive mindset. Keep in mind there is always someone worse off than you. "Every good gift and every perfect gift is from above, coming down from the Father of lights, with whom there is no variation or shadow due to change" (James 1:17).
2. Pray and ask the Lord for strength and wisdom. Remember, there is nothing too big for God to handle. And also, be aware that the Lord is not a genie in a bottle. But if you are sincere and ask Him for wisdom and strength, He will come through and help you. But you must ask for it from Him. "Do not be anxious about anything, but in everything by prayer and supplication with thanksgiving let your requests be made known to God" (Philippians 4:6).
3. Let God do the heavy lifting. Do your part and allow Christ to do what He does best. If He wants you to help someone in need, then do it. If He wants you to stop and visit someone in the hospital, then obey Him. Do what He directs, and He will come through in a mighty big way.

4. Resist discouraging thoughts. When the devil sends them your way, pray, seek counsel, listen to Christian songs, or do an activity to help get your mind off those thoughts. Play a round of golf with some friends or hold a Fantasy Football draft. The devil will throw those thoughts at you because He wants to sack you. Fend off the blitz and opt for a screen play. "The one who offers thanksgiving as his sacrifice glorifies me; to one who orders his way rightly I will show the salvation of God!" (Psalm 50:23).
5. Praise and thank God often. Do this in the good and bad times. When you can worship the Lord in difficult circumstances, then imagine the blessings in the good times. No matter what, God is the Lord of lords and King of kings. He is your Savior in all circumstances. Praise Him through it all without expectations. "The LORD is my strength and my shield; in him my heart trusts, and I am helped; my heart exults, and with my song I give thanks to him" (Psalm 28:7).

Attitude is everything. How you handle difficult or challenging times will tell a lot about you. It will also be an opportunity for God to show Himself to you. But He may be hesitant if you are not in tune with Him. Your faith and positive mindset will be more beneficial than a doom-and-gloom outlook. Never let the devil bring you down to his level. Just ask yourself where would you be without the Lord.

Chapter 7

WELCOME BACK

Levi Wallace
Cornerback

Not everyone who says to me, "Lord, Lord," will enter the kingdom of heaven, but the one who does the will of my Father who is in heaven.

—Matthew 7:21

Just because you might have grown up in church doesn't mean you cannot go astray in your walk with Christ. No one plans to do this, but it can and does happen. Just like a football player can walk off the field and quit, so a believer can stray from his or her journey with the Lord.

The Lord loves you and wants the best for you. He does not send anyone to hell. Your decisions do that for Him. He gave you the freedom to make your own decisions. Free will. What a marvelous invention with wonderful or treacherous results. Levi knew this when he drifted from Jesus.

"I grew up in church and in a Christian home and always went to church," he said. "If the door was open, we were there. Two or three times a week, Christmas plays, Easter plays, youth groups. I stayed in church all the time. It was all I knew."

The Tucson, Arizona, native was a high school standout, and his ability caught the attention of Alabama head football coach Nick Saban. But that's when Levi started down an uncharted highway, where he lost sight of God. The Lord never left, but Levi wandered off course.

"Going into Bama, that was the year I lost my dad," he said. "I kind of rejected my faith for a couple of years. I knew I was lost. I knew it was wrong. I just felt alone when I rejected Him after my dad died. I was just upset and angry about losing my dad at a young age. I kind of just thought I could take care of myself."

Levi was wrong. He did not see the field his freshman or sophomore year at Alabama. In 2016, he earned a walk-on scholarship for his junior year and played in six games. That was the year he came back to the Lord and started over with his faith.

"I had to make that decision for me," Levi said. "I came back and got baptized again—for the second time, but it felt even better than the first time. God took me back."

In 2018, he started and played a big part in the Crimson Tide's College Football Playoff National Championship 26–23 win over Georgia.

"Looking back, I think I had to go through some of those struggles to appreciate God and my faith," he said. "I left it and walked away for a while. Now Jesus is my Lord and Savior. He never left me, I left Him, but He welcomed me back. I asked

Him for forgiveness, and He gave it to me. I didn't deserve it, but I took it anyway."

During his senior year at Bama, Levi had forty-eight tackles and three interceptions, and it culminated with a championship ring.

"Jesus is everything to me," he added. "He is the reason I have what I have. I know I wouldn't be here or happy without Him."

Return, O faithless sons; I will heal your faithlessness. Behold, we come to you, for you are the LORD our God.
—Jeremiah 3:22

4th and Goal

Has something happened to you that caused you to be irritated with God? Even though the Lord is not to blame, you still find a cause to direct your anger at Him. He is an easy target. Who else can you blame? Right? Maybe you lost someone close to you at a vulnerable age. Perhaps you lost your job for no good reason. Or maybe you are struggling because you've been diagnosed with a serious illness. Or perhaps you were involved in a tragic collision or a natural disaster. No matter what transpired, certain events have caused you to drift away from your faith instead of drawing closer. This is your choice. You have free will.

Touchdown

Discouragement is real. Anger is real. Bitterness is real. When all those come together, the devil laughs because he has you right where he wants you—weak and vulnerable. Sometimes it happens fast, but most of the time people can slowly drift away from God's presence. Here are some actions, or lack of, to warn you that you may be backsliding from the Lord.

1. You stop reading the Bible. Suddenly, you don't take time to read His daily instructions for you. A football player won't make it on the field if he doesn't know the playbook. The same goes for you as a Christian. The Bible is God's love letter to you. There are parts you may not understand, but you must read the inspired Word of God. It's food for your soul and His direction for you on the field. "For the word of God is living and active, sharper than any two-edged sword, piercing to the division of soul and of spirit, of joints and of marrow, and discerning the thoughts and intentions of the heart" (Hebrews 4:12).
2. You stop praying. How would you feel if your spouse or kids quit talking to you? Imagine how the Lord feels when you ignore Him. When you stop praying, you cause distance between you and your heavenly Father. You may not notice immediately, but God does. "Seek the LORD and his strength; seek his presence continually!" (1 Chronicles 16:11).
3. You slack off going to church. How can a football player be effective if he does not show up on the field? God's house is where you find strength and fellowship. Regular church attendance is as important as showing up for work or practice every day. When you slack off

and stop going to church, you drift away from your friends and those who may hold you accountable.

4. You change priorities. Instead of doing the right thing, you become lazy or put events in front of church services. You may find yourself distant from things that were once important to you. "I walk in the way of righteousness, in the paths of justice, granting an inheritance to those who love me, and filling their treasuries. 'The LORD possessed me at the beginning of his work, the first of his acts of old'" (Proverbs 8:20–22).

5. You go places you should not go. Rebellion and sin will take you further than you ever want to go. "Abstain from every form of evil" (1 Thessalonians 5:22).

Levi realized he was wrong and made the decision to come back to the Lord. He blamed God for the death of his dad and took his anger out on Christ. Instead of relying on grace and mercy, he chose to be alone and allow the devil to creep into his life. Don't make the same choice. When times get tough, draw closer. Read your Bible. Pray every day. Stay in church. Keep your priorities straight and stay away from places you should not go. It's that easy.

Chapter 8

GOD IS GREATER THAN . . .

Logan Wilson
Linebacker

Thine, O LORD is the greatness, and the power, and the glory, and the victory, and the majesty: for all that is in the heaven and in the earth is thine; thine is the kingdom, O LORD, and thou art exalted as head above all.
—1 Chronicles 29:11 KJV

Logan is a fundamentally sound and effective linebacker. He is known for his gritty play on the field and all-around hustle. He makes plays when his team needs him to.

In Super Bowl LVI, he was on the negative end of a controversial holding call that resulted in the Los Angeles Rams defeating the Cincinnati Bengals. The result was not his fault, but the Bengals lost their bid to win the league's biggest game.

"I always look for the positives in the game," he said. "I'm healthy and not too banged up. When you have that faith through Christ you can look at those little things and be positive about it. At the end of the day, we still want to win, but we will move on. Losing a game is tough, but it's not the end of the world."

Even though he wants to win every Sunday on the field, he knows there is a greater cause in life. He is aware that he is more than a football player.

"I have a family member who lost a child to SIDS (sudden infant death syndrome) and from an outsiders' perspective, you watch how they handled it," Logan said. "I saw that their faith was in Christ, and they leaned on God to help them heal and go through it with the Lord. I don't think they would have been able to get through it without God and His faithfulness. They are huge role models to me. Losing a kid is more devastating than losing a game."

Adversity will either drive you away from Jesus or lead you closer to Him. That is why Logan has a tattoo on his arm—the same arm he uses to bring down running backs and quarterbacks.

Have I not commanded thee? Be strong and of a good courage; be not afraid, neither be thou dismayed: for the LORD thy God is with thee whithersoever thou goest.
—Joshua 1:9 KJV

"That verse really means a lot to me," he said. "When I was drafted, I didn't even know where Cincinnati was. When I got here, it was the farthest I'd ever been away from home. I leaned on that verse, and it's been a big inspiration for me. I try to live by it every single day. I had no idea where I was going, but I knew that if I trusted God, it would all be OK."

No matter if you travel far away from home or face a difficult situation or tragedy, God and His love for you is greater than anything you'll see.

> *For God so loved the world, that he gave his only begotten Son, that whosoever believeth in him should not perish, but have everlasting life.*
> —John 3:16 KJV

4th and Goal

What are you afraid of? That's a loaded question. Fear is such a great motivator. It's described as an unpleasant emotion that is caused by a belief that something or someone is dangerous and will cause harm or pain or is a threat to you. There are many factors that can invite fear and worry. You've probably been told never to worry. That's easy to say. But in reality, it's a difficult task, especially when life calls. For example, it might be hard not to worry if you have a child in the hospital who is very sick. Or perhaps it may be a challenge not to worry if your job is on the line and you have financial obligations. The future is uncertain and you may have a lot on the line.

Touchdown

It takes a strong trust in God's plan in your life to maintain a positive attitude. In the Bible, Job lost all he had but kept his eyes on the Lord. He endured. He struggled. He was tempted. But he stayed the course. If anyone had a reason to quit, it was Job. Scripture never once referred to him as being afraid.

That's incredible. He knew that His God would deliver him from lousy situations. When fear comes upon you, how do you react? There are several things the devil wants you to fear. Here are some ways to battle those real emotions.

1. Fear of rejection. Everyone wants to be accepted and loved. Rejection can come in many ways. You can be rejected in a personal or romantic relationship. People you thought of as friends can turn their backs on you. But it's true that God will always be there. Even when you cannot see Him, you can see the results. Even when you cannot hear Him, He can whisper sweet peace. "To the praise of the glory of his grace, wherein he hath made us accepted in the beloved" (Ephesians 1:6 KJV).
2. Fear of failure. This can come about by lofty expectations. Today's society has placed a tremendous priority on making it to the top professionally. The fear of letting others down can be considered failure. This can also bring on feelings of depression and discouragement. When this happens, Satan goes in for the sack. He doesn't care about the unsportsmanlike conduct calls. He simply laughs those off. As long as you serve the Lord with all your heart and soul, you will be a winner. Failure happens when you give up. Keep going. At the end of the game, you will receive your MVP award. "But thanks be to God, which giveth us the victory through our Lord Jesus Christ" (1 Corinthians 15:57 KJV).
3. Fear of being alone. You are human and have a natural affinity for a community. When you are left alone,

you feel helpless and afraid. Who will be there for you? When those you expected to stay by your side abandon you, then you feel vulnerable. You feel like a target. A lion prefers to separate the pack and find the one who cannot defend itself. The Lord will stick by you when others leave. "And David said to Solomon his son, Be strong and of good courage, and do it: fear not, nor be dismayed: for the Lord God, even my God, will be with thee; he will not fail thee, nor forsake thee, until thou hast finished all the work for the service of the house of the Lord" (1 Chronicles 28:20 KJV).

4. Fear of the unknown. This might be the worst of all. When you don't know, you have a tendency to be scared of the future. What will happen when the doctor comes in tomorrow? What will the test results show next week? How will you make ends meet and pay bills without a job? Will your kids be OK when you're gone?
5. Fear of fear. Life is meant to be enjoyed. Happiness is your choice. You can spend your life in paranoia or in the confidence that you are saved to the uttermost. "Make me to hear joy and gladness; that the bones which thou hast broken may rejoice" (Psalm 51:8 KJV).

God is greater than rejection. God is greater than failure. God is greater than loneliness. God is greater than the unknown. God is greater than fear. God is greater than . . .

Chapter 9

GOD LOVES YOU!

Jessie Bates III
All-Pro Safety

Do your best to present yourself to God as one approved, a worker who has no need to be ashamed, rightly handling the word of truth.

—2 Timothy 2:15

Believe it or not, there are times when a professional football player feels unwanted or rejected. The money doesn't matter. The lavish lifestyle is not enough. Fancy cars and shiny jewelry seem irrelevant at times. Those are the trademarks of some players, but what they really want is to be wanted and needed.

A player in the NFL wants comaraderie and to belong. He has a desire to be included and wanted on a roster. The feeling of "belonging" is vital to the athlete. It means more than physical stature or awards.

There have been many stories about former players who feel lost without the locker room. They become discouraged and depressed because they have lost their identities as athletes. Some have slipped into despair and lost all they had accumulated because they lost their way when they were released. They lost their community and the sense of belonging.

Jessie went through a time before the 2022 season when he did not feel the Cincinnati Bengals wanted him. He had just come off the exciting playoff run with the Bengals and recorded his second playoff interception when he picked off Los Angeles Rams quarterback Matthew Stafford in the endzone in Super Bowl LVI.

In March 2022, Cincinnati placed the franchise tag on him, and he signed the deal in August, just in time for the season. He was not thrilled but inked his name.

"For me, I just kind of felt like I was not wanted as much," he said. "You go back and read the Word and the Bible, and you just trust your faith. You are loved, and you are enough. God just kept telling me that. He's madly in love with you and me, and that kind of stuff can't change. His love for me is so big. And my faith shouldn't change, and the fact that God loves you will never change. Teams will come and go and at times you might feel unwanted, but God will always want you."

Jessie has learned to tiptoe the sidelines and juggle the pins of confidence, humility, and gratitude all at the same time.

"In this game, it kind of blows your mind because it's all about performance," he added. "It's all about winning, making the plays, success, and stuff like that. There is a lot of pressure to perform at the highest level. And at the same time, you have to trust your faith and ability that you are enough. That's where God comes in. He tells me I'm enough. Coaches and brass and media look at stats and big plays, but God doesn't do that. I know I am enough for Him, and He is more than enough for me."

The 2018 second-round NFL Draft pick and product of Wake Forest noted that one big key to his success off the field is to surround himself with like-minded people. That encourages him and feeds his human desire to feel wanted.

"You just have to have a strong support system," he said. "Especially those who will help you spiritually. I surround myself with people of faith who inspire me. That's important in this game. Guys who will pray with each other. I mean guys who get down on their knees and seek God's face. I want to make sure I do my part because I know God has done His. He tells me every day that He loves me."

Jesus Christ is the same yesterday and today and forever.
—Hebrews 13:8

4th and Goal

Have you ever felt unwanted? Has someone made remarks to you, or about you, that caused you to feel lousy about yourself? Maybe you were passed over for a job promotion or an incident propelled you to become the target of someone's poor sense of humor. Perhaps you were humiliated in front of someone you admire. Or maybe a relationship went south, and you feel less than desirable. Society also plays a tremendous role in tearing down your self-esteem. Social media has poisoned expectations and promotes glamour and good looks over sincerity and character.

Touchdown

Never lose sight that God loves you, just the way you are. He sent His Son to the cross to die for your sins and for you. That can slip your mind when people make fun of you. People can be cruel with words and actions and it's human nature to defend yourself against attacks. It's easy to say turn the other cheek but difficult to follow through. However, it is the best course to take. When the storms of life surround you, try your best to seek God and find comfort in Him. Here are some ways to always know that the Lord loves you.

1. God created you. He did not make a mistake when you were conceived and born. He has specific plans for you. This may seem hard to fathom when things get tough but remember to look at the big picture. He will do a work for you when you surrender your all to Him. He wants the best for you. Always remember that. "Do you not know that you are God's temple and that God's Spirit dwells in you?" (1 Corinthians 3:16).
2. He died for you. This is the ultimate sacrifice. You are that important to Him. He would not have sent Jesus to die for your sins if you did not have value and a purpose. The fact that Christ was crucified for you sends the message that you are precious in His sight. "But God shows his love for us in that while we were still sinners, Christ died for us" (Romans 5:8).
3. He conquered death for you. This is the only way to

heaven. There are many people who will not enter the Kingdom because they have not accepted Christ and invited Him into their hearts. Never take this for granted or view it lightly. This is huge. You can live forever with Him. That's amazing.

4. He will provide for you. You may not see it now, but He does have a plan and will not allow you to fail if you stay in His will. Life just seems to work out in the end. You may question why something is happening and be confused, but God is working on your behalf. One of the hardest things to do is wait on His plan. He is preparing you for the right moment. "Consider the ravens: they neither sow nor reap, they have neither storehouse nor barn, and yet God feeds them. Of how much more value are you than the birds!" (Luke 12:24).

5. He has prepared heaven for you. What better place to spend eternity? He loves you enough to want to spend forever with you. "But, as it is written, 'What no eye has seen, nor ear heard, nor the heart of man imagined, what God has prepared for those who love him'" (1 Corinthians 2:9).

Jessie noted that he felt unwanted during contract negotiations. He wanted to feel valued for his ability and not like a piece of property. But he never lost sight that God loves him. God loves you too. He loves you just as much as He loves Jessie. He loves you as much and wants the best for you. Always remember that when doubt creeps into your mind. You are valuable on His roster and worth the life of Jesus Christ.

Chapter 10

WHAT IS GOD TEACHING YOU?

Johnny Hekker
All-Pro Punter

And without faith it is impossible to please him, for whoever would draw near to God must believe that he exists and that he rewards those who seek him.

—Hebrews 11:6

Johnny kicks a football for a living. And he does it well. The Oregon State product has earned All-Pro status more than once and been selected to a few Pro Bowls. He played a big part on the Los Angeles Rams team that won Super Bowl LVI, and he was chosen to be on the roster for the NFL 2010s All-Decade Team.

In 2021, he punted the football fifty-one times for 2,252 yards. Twenty-three of those kicks were downed inside the other team's twenty-yard line. That is impressive and a special teams coach's dream.

During the Wild Card Round against the Arizona Cardinals, Johnny planted all five of his punts inside the twenty-yard line, which won the battle of field position. That performance helped the Rams win and advance in the playoffs. In Super Bowl LVI, he punted six times against the Cincinnati Bengals for a whopping 261 yards. Despite that magical season and a Super Bowl win, he was released by the Rams the next month.

"I struggle with doubt and fear," he said. "Being a football player, a lot of your identity and self-worth can be wrapped up in your performance. Sometimes, when I have a hard day or a hard year, or a hard little while in my career, I can be critical and think to myself, *What's going on here, God? What are you trying to teach me? Am I being punished for something?* It can drive me crazy because it stays in my mind and thoughts."

The Lord won't punish, but instead He might put you in a position where you can learn and grow for your betterment.

"Really, there is a refining that is being done by the Holy Spirit," Johnny added. "That's when I realize that God is using those times to give me a better platform to reach those who are in a similar situation and whatever their walk of life is at that particular time. That's what is going on, but it can be hard to remember that in tough times."

When confusion presents itself, the intention is to create doubt. The devil is the author of confusion and takes delight when a child of God questions the Lord's existence. He knows that if he can cause doubt, he has a chance to sack you for a big loss.

"Faith is acknowledging that you would not be where you are without God's grace," Johnny said. "He provides for me.

He's always provided for me. I look back on some of the crazy twists and turns of my career and my life up to that point—or even making the NFL and much less being where I am now."

For Johnny, his productive NFL career has been one miracle after another.

"I've had some tough points where I've had to look back at how I'm really living and how I am going to overcome some adversity," he said. "I just realize that God has never left my side through it all—and He's been with me through it all and has blessed me with so much through the process. I'm just grateful and just want to shine some glory on Him."

Maybe God was teaching him to trust His plan.

For we walk by faith, not by sight.
—2 Corinthians 5:7

4th and Goal

Having feelings of doubt or confusion probably has happened to you or someone you know. Now, this is not referring to you as an All-Pro punter and being released after winning a Super Bowl, but life is unpredictable. Maybe you won major awards at work and earned a promotion only to be released or downsized. Or perhaps you've made healthy choices in your diet and exercise and have received discouraging news from your doctor about your health. Or maybe you've been in a long relationship with hopes of a future together only to see it crumble before your eyes.

Touchdown

Trusting God is easy, right? It should be, but everyone has struggles with faith. If you nodded your head to that statement, then you're not alone. When life is going great and then dark days come and cover you with a sense of uncertainty, you might have brief moments of doubts and question God: *What is going on?* Here are some ways to trust Christ's plan during confusing times.

1. Relinquish your plans for His plan. The worst thing you can do is make plans for your life that are *not* from the will of God. Remember, your life is not about you, but it's about how you can glorify the Father. It's OK to have dreams and aspirations and prepare in advance for a good life. But you must allow the Holy Spirit to lead you. If your doors keep closing, then stop trying to open them on your own. Let loose of control. "For I know the plans I have for you, declares the Lord, plans for welfare and not for evil, to give you a future and a hope" (Jeremiah 29:11).
2. Keep your focus on the ultimate destination. If you know you're going to take a wonderful vacation but must travel through some rough roads, that motivates you to keep going. When life takes a bizarre turn, don't let your eyes turn away from your final destination. Focus on where you are going and not what you are going through. "Therefore, since we are surrounded by so great a cloud of witnesses, let us also lay aside every weight, and sin which clings so closely, and let us run

with endurance the race that is set before us" (Hebrews 12:1).

3. Prepare for the unexpected. Professional athletes go through rigorous training in the offseason. Hours and hours of preparation is essential for them to compete at the highest level when the season begins. You must do the same. You have to read your Bible every day. You must pray, talk, and listen to Jesus every day. You need to attend church on a regular basis. This will help prepare you for everyday situations. Never expect anything for your preparation but instead be ready for what life tosses at you.

4. Expect Him to provide. Imagine that your favorite team is behind by six points with two minutes to go in the game. You get nervous and tense up, but you believe the quarterback will lead the team down the field for the come-from-behind win. You trust. You expect. The same goes for you when you are faced with unforeseen circumstances. Expect a miracle. Never bargain with the Lord but believe He has the best intentions for you. Worship Him and ask for a miracle. "Truly, truly, I say to you, whoever believes in me will also do the works that I do; and greater works than these will he do, because I am going to the Father" (John 14:12).

5. Praise and worship more than ever. In good and bad times, lift up the name of Christ. Praise Him for what He has done and for what He will do for you in the future. See the good in your situations and grow spiritually. "I will sing to the LORD as long as I live; I will sing praise to my God while I have being" (Psalm 104:33).

When you travel down a narrow road, it is never easy. It causes you to grip the wheel and sit closer on the seat. But if you stay the course and trust the vehicle and keep calm and focused, you'll make it. You can live a life filled with joy and peace and gratefulness. It's OK to plan but roll with the flow if the Lord changes your plans for His.

Chapter 11

BE A BETTER PERSON

Trey Hendrickson
Pro Bowl Defensive End

Iron sharpens iron, and one man sharpens another.
—Proverbs 27:17

Trey had the pleasure of being raised by Christian parents who inspired him to make a commitment of faith. The Pro Bowl defensive end was taught values and encouraged to live for the Lord, but he had to make his own choice. His faith was not inherited.

When the Orlando, Florida, native played football at Florida Atlantic, he grew in his spiritual walk with Christ.

"When you are in college, it's important to have a deep root in your faith," he said. "My parents instilled a lot of core values in me that I could fall back on and lean on in times of trial and darkness and confusion. I was blessed to have been raised that way."

Trey identifies with everyday Christians who have personal issues and problems. Each person's problems are unique to them. What is crucial to you may not seem like a big deal to others. But to you, it's monumental. And to God, it's also a big deal. He cares about you and what troubles you.

"Everyone in life will have adversity and when that adversity comes, and it will, that's when it's great to be able to fall back on Christ—and when you can't carry that burden any more or any longer, you rely on Jesus Christ and that's when you are truly relieved and know that you have a great big God who loves you and He died for you and your sins."

When those tough times come, it's also important to have a friend to confide in and lean on. If you are blessed to have this resource, then never take it for granted.

"My wife pushes me to be a better man every day," Trey said. "She also helps me to be a better teammate too. Every day we meditate and pray together—a lot. She has my back no matter what. That brings a different element to me. It's all about faith, family, and football."

If you have a spouse who inspires you, then try to do the same in return. If you do not, then try to find a band of people who are like-minded and want to encourage you.

"My mom is still my inspiration, because she just loves Jesus," he added. "She is such a great woman, and I owe everything I am to her and everything that is good in me to her."

Trey is also quite the football player. He makes his presence known on the field every week. In week 3 of the 2022 season, he had four tackles, forced two fumbles, and had a pair of sacks for the Cincinnati Bengals in a 27–12 win over the

New York Jets. That performance earned him AFC Defensive Player of the Week.

"I was taught to try hard in everything I do, and that's because my parents instilled a good work ethic in me," he said. "They taught me to give it everything I have, and they encouraged me to follow Christ."

> *One generation shall commend your works to another, and shall declare your mighty acts.*
>
> —Psalm 145:4

4th and Goal

Who pushes you to be better? Who do *you* push? Everyone needs encouragement and motivation. And most people can notice those times when you need a little incentive. But there may be instances in which you may feel alone and discouraged, and no one may notice. And you might be a master at hiding those moments. But when it comes down to it, most people have a desire to be a better person. Maybe you have struggled in school to obtain good grades and that brings you down emotionally. Or perhaps you are not happy with your current job and want to advance your career. Who do you turn to for advice? And who do you inspire to do better?

Touchdown

Encouragement is a great motivator. It goes straight to the heart and gives you a boost. According to research, the word *encourage* has a significant meaning. The first two letters, *en*, mean "to put into" in Latin. And three of the next four letters, *cor*, mean "heart." To put into heart, or encourage. Who can *you* encourage? Who pushes you? Here are some ways you can be the reason someone wants to do better.

1. Send a message or gift. It doesn't take long to send a text message of encouragement to a friend who may be down. You can also send some flowers or a small gift to brighten a person's day. You never need to say much. It's the act that carries the weight. When you tell a friend or your spouse how much they mean to you or that you are thinking of them, it brightens their day. But when you take time to send a handwritten note, it means a lot. Encourage someone today. "For this is the message that you have heard from the beginning, that we should love one another" (1 John 3:11).
2. Remind them of God's promises. When your friends get discouraged, remind them that the Lord will always be there for them. And you can illustrate the point by telling them that is why you are there for them. God sent you to help them through the tough time. "Therefore I intend always to remind you of these qualities, though you know them and are established in the truth that you have" (2 Peter 1:12).
3. Reinforce their faith by praying for them. And don't just say, "I'll pray for you," and leave it at that. Actually, do it—right then and there. If you're on the phone with them, pray. If you are having a cup of coffee, put your hand on their shoulder and pray. Be specific when you pray and praise God for what He is going to do.

"Therefore I intend always to remind you of these qualities, though you know them and are established in the truth that you have" (2 Peter 1:12).
4. Celebrate your friends or spouse. If something positive happens, celebrate with them. You don't need confetti, but make a call and congratulate them, or make a post on social media lifting up the person's accomplishment. "You make known to me the path of life; in your presence there is fullness of joy; at your right hand are pleasures forevermore" (Psalm 16:11).
5. Be there. This is perhaps the best thing you can do. Be present. A hug. A smile. A prayer. A slap on the back. A tear. A laugh. When you make someone feel special and important, you can present the love of God to them in a soft and compassionate way.

Trey's wife pushes him to be better. If you have a spouse, then motivate and encourage them. Pray with them on a regular basis. Celebrate them and make them feel special. Be there for them through the good times and bad ones. Because if you are there, the bad times will get better.

Chapter 12

FIND YOUR VERSE FOR LIFE

Mike Hilton
Cornerback

These things I have spoken unto you, that in me ye might have peace. In the world ye shall have tribulation: but be of good cheer; I have overcome the world.
—John 16:33 KJV

Coming out of Ole Miss, Mike was projected by NFL experts and scouts to go undrafted and be a free agent. Although very talented, the 5-foot-9-inch wide receiver from Fayetteville, Georgia, did not receive an invitation to the NFL combine but attended the University of Mississippi pro day in March 2016. He was determined to make it.

Mike was ranked the twenty-seventh best free safety prospect in the draft by NFLDraftScout.com. But he received many positive reviews from scouts for his ability to play more than one position. He possessed good coverage skills and was noted as a gritty tackler and demonstrated quick foot speed.

He had an uncanny way to track balls downfield, but most saw his smaller size as a deterrent in the draft.

He signed as a free agent with Jacksonville in May 2016 but was released before the season started. Four months later he inked a deal with the New England Patriots. But Mike was released about a week later and signed on with the Pittsburgh Steelers three months later in December. On March 19, 2021, he signed a four-year deal with the Cincinnati Bengals where he made an impact and found a home.

"When I went undrafted, that was hard and tough," Mike said. "Then, chances to make the team were slim. But you know I just kept believing and trusting in Him. I kept praying and asking and kept putting in the work on my end. I knew my time would come. It was hard to wait but I knew God had my back and had good things in store for me."

Mike leaned on Philippians 4:13, which stresses that "I can do all things through Christ which strengtheneth me." He never forgot the message in that inspirational verse.

"Believing in Christ and for what He provides really means something special to me," he added. "Through the good and bad times, He's got your back. I just love that scripture. It means so much to me."

Mike grew up in church. That was all he knew and how he was raised.

"That's what I want to pass down to my kids," he said. "There is just something special about it. Living that way and believing in Jesus Christ is the best life. It's the best because knowing there is more to life . . . you know things that may not always be right or the way you want them. But if you put your trust in the Lord then things will work out in your favor. I'm living proof of that."

Mike leaned on his favorite verse for strength. What verse do you fall back on for inspiration? What helps get you through tough times?

> *Now the God of hope fill you with all joy and peace in believing, that ye may abound in hope, through the power of the Holy Ghost.*
> —Romans 15:13 KJV

4th and Goal

What brings you motivation when you face challenging times? Is it a song? A quote from a movie? Is there a secret hiding place no one knows about? Some people fall back on quotes from C. S. Lewis or Charles Spurgeon. John Wayne has a fabulous quote that can bring comfort. The Duke once said, "Life is hard. It's harder if you're stupid." Charles M. Schulz, the famed creator of the *Peanuts* gang and Snoopy said, "I love humanity. It's people I can't stand."

Touchdown

Whatever brings you inspiration or works for you in this area should be noted. But it's also important to find a biblical verse to fit you as a person. This is not mandatory, but it can be helpful. It can be your motto or anthem for life. Here are some popular verses and what they can do for you when you are in a struggle. A life verse can be one or two lines of scripture that speak to you as a person in a profound way. Your life verse should draw you closer to the Lord and remind you of His unconditional love for you. Pray about it and be sure to read the Bible every day. If you can't locate one, then don't force the issue. Write down or journal your thoughts. The more you read the Scriptures, the more you are exposed to His thoughts. Your life verse can change, or it can be a mainstay throughout your journey. Here are some suggested verses to consider when finding your life verse.

1. Romans 8:28: "And we know that all things work together for good to them that love God, to them who are the called according to his purpose" (KJV). This means that God works for the good of those who love Him. You can trust that He is working for your good. He loves you. You have been called by Him for a purpose that He holds for your life.
2. Matthew 5:16: "Let your light so shine before men, that they may see your good works, and glorify your Father which is in heaven" (KJV). Jesus said that your good deed should be seen and noticed. You are encouraged to fast and pray for opportunities to let your light shine. The focus here is to bring glory and honor to Him. Sometimes you will be praised by others, but that should not be your intent. If it happens it's OK, but the glory needs to be redirected back to the Lord. It's not the action, but the attitude of the heart that is important and what God wants to see.
3. Matthew 6:33: "But seek ye first the kingdom of God, and his righteousness; and all these things shall be

added unto you" (KJV). This means you need to focus your life goals on what He wants you to do. You might have plans, but the Lord may have something else in mind for you. God in His grace invites you to live a life that is free from worry and anxiety. If you make life decisions or plans without seeking God's face first, then those plans might go down in flames. Seek Him first.

4. John 8:12: "Then spake Jesus again unto them, saying, I am the light of the world: he that followeth me shall not walk in darkness, but shall have the light of life" (KJV). This means that no matter what happens in your life, God will always be the light. You will go through problems and issues you think are too hard, but when you trust in Him, you will have peace and you will be able to find your way.

5. Joshua 1:9: "Have not I commanded thee? Be strong and of a good courage; be not afraid, neither be thou dismayed: for the LORD thy God is with thee whithersoever thou goest" (KJV). If you trust in the Father, you *will* make it. Don't be discouraged or anxious. If you lose your job or receive troubling news from a doctor, then cling to His promise.

Mike held on to the popular Philippians 4:13 when he was not selected in the NFL Draft. But he made it through hard work and prayer. There are thousands of verses to pick for a life verse. But the point here is to find one that fits you. God made you and loves you. He has a verse for you too.

Chapter 13

LET THEM SEE JESUS

Diontae Johnson
All-Pro Wide Receiver

For by grace you have been saved through faith. And this is not your own doing; it is the gift of God, not a result of works, so that no one may boast.
—Ephesians 2:8–9

Diontae's sophomore year at Toledo was a challenging time. He had to retake the ACT, a standardized test for college admission, and he underwent surgery on his foot. After a solid and productive freshman season in 2015 with the Rockets, the sophomore year seemed like it was going to last forever. He was not sure he wanted to continue pursuing football. He just wasn't confident about anything.

"That was a tough time in my life," he said. "I had to retake a test and then sit out because of surgery. I couldn't do anything with the team. I just wanted to go home and give up."

But during that lonely time, he found what he needed. It wasn't football. It wasn't on a field of play. It wasn't in the locker room. Diontae found his way to the house of the Lord.

"I was saved my sophomore year," he said. "I was so down and discouraged and didn't know if I would ever play again during that time. I didn't feel like I had a team or anyone on my side. I had to go to church and find God. That's what I needed all the time. It was there waiting on me."

It was the best catch he would ever make. God was there, waiting on Diontae to shake off the defense and get open. The next year on the field in 2017, Diontae had seventy-four receptions with 1,278 yards with thirteen touchdowns in fourteen games. He finished his career with 2,235 yards receiving with twenty-three touchdowns and was chosen First Team All-Mid-American Conference in 2017 and 2018.

The Pittsburgh Steelers drafted him in the third round of the 2019 NFL Draft. And to think, he considered giving it all up when he was forced to sit out for a while in college.

"I cannot do anything without Him—without God in my life," he said. "All my success I give to Him every day. I can't wake up without giving Him the glory and honor. Even before I step onto the field, I have to give Him the credit.

"I was around the team pastor and that helped me—I could always go talk to him and get some courage and knowledge."

Diontae lets everyone know how he feels about the Lord. He doesn't hesitate or back down when it comes to the Lord.

"It's not about how much faith you have, it's about *who* your faith is in," he Tweeted on September 19, 2021. About one month later, he Tweeted out, "When God gives you a dream, the dream will always be tested."

"My belief is that without God in my life, I am nothing," he added. "But with Him, I know I can do anything, as long as I let Him guide me."

Diontae's NFL goals include catching touchdown passes and winning a Super Bowl, but his main focus in life is to grow closer to Christ.

"I want to get closer to the Lord," he said. "As I get older, it gets more real. I still try to get closer to Him each day. I have to draw closer. I go to church and pray and read my Bible a lot."

He is public with his faith, which helps him stay strong in his walk as a Christian.

"I try to watch what I post on social media because you never know who is following," he added. "If I see a kid wanting an autograph, I try to go out there and sign it—whoever it is—and give some words of wisdom and inspiration and determination to them. I want them to see Jesus in me."

Because, if you confess with your mouth that Jesus is Lord and believe in your heart that God raised him from the dead, you will be saved.

—Romans 10:9

4th and Goal

Has something happened in your life that left you confused or scared? If so, then you are not alone. Have you been forced to retake an important test or sit out on the sideline and watch the world go by? The test may not be academic, but it may be a medical procedure. Maybe your career is off to a slow start. Or perhaps you feel abandoned and alone. Do you have that special relationship with Jesus to lead you through the storm? Do you feel the need to get closer to the Master?

Touchdown

It's human nature to want to draw closer to those you love. If you have a special person in your life whom you love, you want to find comfort with them in times of struggle. If you have a cute puppy, you find the time to snuggle and cuddle with it. There are ways and tools you can use to draw closer to the Lord to help you in your spiritual life. There are the usuals you can do: read your Bible, pray, go to church, worship more—all of those are fundamental and work. But here are some other ways you can snuggle up and cuddle with the Lord.

1. Memorize scripture. This will help you in daily battles. It's human nature to sin. But if you are equipped with scripture, you can fend off the devil's blitzes and reach the line to gain. Start off with short and simple verses to give yourself confidence. Have a goal of one new verse per week. "All Scripture is breathed out by God and profitable for teaching, for reproof, for correction, and for training in righteousness" (2 Timothy 3:16).
2. Get in shape. You don't have to be Charles Atlas, but you can honor the Lord by maintaining the temple He gave you. Take care of yourself the best you can and avoid putting junk into your body. This might include abstaining from alcohol and tobacco. Food can also be an addiction, and gluttony is a sin. Be careful what you take in as a food source. "Or do you not know that your body is a temple of the Holy Spirit within you,

whom you have from God? You are not your own, for you were bought with a price. So glorify God in your body" (1 Corinthians 6:19–20).

3. Practice humility. When you are humble, you allow yourself to be used by God. The Lord will not call you to do something if you are arrogant or full of pride. In Proverbs 3:34, God's Word says He will give you favor if you are filled with humility.
4. Fast. When you give up something you enjoy or need to praise the Lord, God will honor that and draw closer to you. This does not mean you use Christ as a wishing well. You fast because you want to be used for the glory of the Kingdom. "So we fasted and implored our God for this, and he listened to our entreaty" (Ezra 8:23).
5. Do good. Show kindness. Show respect for authority. Volunteer your time. Be honest in all you do. These are expected but when they are carried out, you will find yourself in favor with the Lord. Remember that you are not saved because of works or deeds, but they go hand-in-hand with the Christian walk.

No one is perfect and you will make mistakes along the way. There will be times of discouragement and times of doubt and trouble. Just make sure those times are few and far between and short. But when those moments arrive, draw closer to the Lord.

Chapter 14

BE THE MAN

Chase Edmonds
Running Back

*And the L*ORD *said unto Satan, Hast thou considered my servant Job, that there is none like him in the earth, a perfect and an upright man, one that feareth God, and escheweth evil?*
—Job 1:8 KJV

The devil wants you to fail in life. He wants to sack you and force a fumble deep in your own territory. He will not play fair. Satan will jump offsides. He will hold you at all costs and then grab your facemask and bring you hard to the turf. There are no rules when it comes to the forces of evil.

The devil wants you to quit. He will not give up until he has met his match . . . and that is *not* you. By yourself, you are no competition for the devil. He knows this. Chase also knows this and that is why one of his favorite accounts from the Bible is Job.

"I like him because life is all about trials and tribulations," he said. "Job was the man. He lived a great life and had all the land and a beautiful family. He had the cattle and everything he needed. And then the devil goes to God and says, 'Job worships you because You give him all these things, like riches and treasures.'"

You are aware of what happens next. Job's world comes crashing down. "God lets the devil play with Job," Chase added. "But God tells the devil that 'you can touch Job. But you cannot kill him. No harm to him.' The devil takes everything Job has. His family. His riches. His cattle. His health. Everything.

"But Job's resilience and his determination is amazing, and he continues to worship God. And eventually, Job gets it all back tenfold. He could have quit—and was encouraged to do that—but he didn't."

Regardless how long Job waited, he knew the Lord would take care of him through it all. His family was taken, and his wealth was attacked. But Job's faith was real. Job knew the One he served. "This is an awesome testament to life in general," Chase said. "You just cannot give up—even when it looks bad. Stay focused on the Lord and He will provide."

> *Behold, God is mighty, and despiseth not any: he is mighty in strength and wisdom.*
>
> —Job 36:5 KJV

4th and Goal

What can you withstand? What trial or tribulation might cause you to consider tossing in the towel? You will be blitzed and blindsided at some point in your life. You may face a devastating health diagnosis or be involved in a serious accident. You may be tossed into unemployment or lose your life savings. Will you have the resilience of Job? He was encouraged to give up and die, but he knew the mighty God of David. He knew the Rose of Sharon. He knew the Master.

Touchdown

The Lord is the *only* way to get through the trials of life. But there are some bad habits you may have been exposed to over the years or throughout your life that may hinder your faith. When you fall into the devil's traps of a certain pattern or routine, he is counting on you to give up and doubt God's power and commitment to you. Here are some patterns the devil wants you to fall into, so you won't possess Job's determination and resilience.

1. Ignorance. The devil will tell you that you do everything needed to be a Christian. You look the part. You go to church and do good all the time. You give to the poor and you toss a few bucks in the offering plate every Sunday. You carry your Bible to Sunday school and bow your head to pray. You put in the time and that's good enough. But you never get into the game because you are not ready. Instead, be prepared and read your Bible every day. Pray to your heavenly Father instead of going through the motions. Find the truth in the Word of God. "Examine yourselves, whether ye be in the faith; prove your own selves. Know ye not your own selves, how that Jesus Christ is in you, except ye be reprobates?" (2 Corinthians 13:5 KJV).

2. Discouragement. The devil uses this one to perfection. It's real and must be dealt with. He will cut your legs out from underneath you and laugh while you roll around in pain. Then he will whisper in your ear to give up and quit. He will pile it on until he gets you into a vulnerable position. Don't fall for this. It's OK to feel discouraged due to life's problems, but don't linger there too long. "Be strong and of a good courage, fear not, nor be afraid of them: for the Lord thy God, he it is that doth go with thee; he will not fail thee, nor forsake thee" (Deuteronomy 31:6 KJV).
3. Indifference. The devil wants you to be consumed with *your* life and yours only. He wants you to be focused on your dreams and ambitions so much that you don't see anything else. You don't notice your spouse or kids. Your job is the most important thing in your life. But God wants the opposite. The Lord wants you to show kindness and forgive others. He calls you to help those in need and to put your own needs last. "But when he saw the multitudes, he was moved with compassion on them, because they fainted, and were scattered abroad, as sheep having no shepherd" (Matthew 9:36 KJV).
4. Laziness. The devil wants someone else to do the right thing—not you. He will put distractions in your day to make sure you stay out of God's will for your life. He will cause you to stay out too late on Saturday, so you'll be too tired to go to the house of the Lord on Sunday. He will tell you the font is too small to read your Bible and he will cause your phone to buzz when you finally feel like praying. This is where you must

have determination no matter what. Carve out time each day to read His letter to you. Put "pray" on your calendar each day and don't stray from it. And finally, attend church on a regular basis. Instead of being lazy, you will become strong.

5. Hopelessness. The devil will tell you that you do not matter. Your life has no value, and no matter what you do, you are not important. He will try to push you down in the sewer through lies and bad relationships. But no matter how far down you go, the Lord will rescue you from despair. There is hope. "My soul fainteth for thy salvation: but I hope in thy word" (Psalm 119:81 KJV).

Chase looked up to Job's experience and got inspiration and motivation from the account. The devil wants to destroy you and will use ignorance, discouragement, indifference, laziness, and hopelessness to drive you into the ground. But make it a point to read Job at least twice a year, or more if needed. It's OK to seek counsel and help if you feel yourself falling into these patterns. But the best thing to do is trust the Lord.

Chapter 15

WHEN PEACE FALLS FROM THE CAR

Cade York
Placekicker

And let the peace of Christ rule in your hearts, to which indeed you were called in one body. And be thankful.
—Colossians 3:15

The life of an NFL kicker is filled with ups and downs. They can be the hero one week and the butt of jokes from fans the next. A quarterback has many attempts during a game to connect with receivers and that's part of the game. But a kicker gets one shot when he trots on the field. He either boots the ball through the uprights or he misses.

Kicking the extra point or a thirty-five-yard field goal looks easy. But the craft is extremely difficult. There is no such thing as a gimmie. And when you add the pressure of making a kick, then it becomes more tense. Cade had that experience in October 2022 when his Cleveland Browns faced off against the Los Angeles Chargers.

Earlier in the season, the LSU product won the game against Carolina. But not this game. On this day he missed two field goals. One from forty-five yards out, and the fifty-four-yard attempt that would have won the game was pushed wide to the right and gave the Chargers a 30–28 win in Cleveland.

Cade was disappointed and struggled with his faith, but later God reminded him to put discouraging news behind him.

"One of the coolest things that happened to me was after the Chargers game, when I missed the game-winner," he said.

How can that be cool?

"That entire week was tough for me, and I was praying and getting frustrated at the same time," he said. "I was asking God for peace and wisdom, and I was like, 'why can't I ever hear from you?'"

Cade wanted a dialogue. But he never heard words.

"I couldn't hear or feel God," he added. "I felt alone."

The 124th pick in the 2022 NFL Draft parked his car and started toward his home, still frustrated and irritated. He jerked open the back door of his car to get something out when God spoke to Cade—in His *own* miraculous way.

"My old journal I forgot about fell out of the car and I [saw] a page from two years ago that I wrote," he said. "It was a sermon I'd heard at church and in bold letters it said 'to forget the past.' It sent chills down my back and all over my body."

He shed some tears when he thought about what he was praying about and his desire to hear from the Lord.

"I look back at that moment and use that as something that can give me peace," he said. "When I go through times of adversity, not only praising Him in times of struggle but also praising Him in my times of success—that is a big thing for me."

Cade did not hear from Christ in audible words but by causing a message he needed to see fall out from his car right in front of him.

Do not be anxious about anything, but in everything by prayer and supplication with thanksgiving let your requests be made known to God.

—Philippians 4:6

4th and Goal

Does God speak to you? Perhaps you need to hear from the Lord and He hasn't made His voice clear. Maybe you are going through a tough week and long for His guidance or comfort. In the Gospel of John, Mary and Martha watched their brother, Lazarus, die. They waited on the Lord but in all accounts, the Master was four days late. But when Jesus arrived, to the astonishment of Mary and Martha, He summoned Lazarus from the tomb. He was now alive. God's timing was perfect.

Touchdown

God is not silent. He still makes His voice heard and His actions seen. The Lord continues to speak to you in different ways. But the biggest and best thing you must do is wait and listen. Most people like to talk and take action. The most difficult thing to do is be quiet and listen. Be grateful that He does speak to you in several ways. Here are a few methods in which God can send you the message you need to hear.

1. Through a crisis or suffering. Hopefully, this won't apply to you, but odds are that it will. God will make His presence known to you via a lousy situation or a crisis. This can be in several forms but the point to this is that God provides peace during the storm. You may not feel Him, but just as Cade found out later, He is there waiting to deliver you in the most appropriate time. Perhaps you are an innocent bystander and you brought on the pain yourself. The Lord will still teach and comfort if you allow it to happen. "You will seek me and find me, when you seek me with all your heart" (Jeremiah 29:13).
2. Through praise and worship. The Master can use music and praise in powerful form. There are many times when some have taken great pleasure in a song. Dove Award–winning gospel singer Karen Peck sang "Four Days Late," which describes when Jesus raised Lazarus from the dead. The song inspires those who are going through tough times and need to hear from the Lord. Great things happen when God is praised in honesty and sincerity. When you need to hear from the Lord, raise your voice and arms instead. You might get the response you desire.
3. Through wise and appropriate counsel. Christ uses pastors and seasoned believers to help through experience and a fresh perspective. When you need encouragement, guidance, or compassion, reach out to your pastor or Sunday school teacher or someone you look up to for spiritual help. God has given you good friends or a spouse who can pray with you. "When the Spirit

of truth comes, he will guide you into all the truth, for he will not speak on his own authority, but whatever he hears he will speak, and he will declare to you the things that are to come" (John 16:13).

4. Through happiness. This does not mean you find the answer through money or pleasures of the world. It means that when you fully trust in the Lord, then He will take care of you. In the first chapter of James, the Bible tells you that every good thing comes from the Lord. When you finally realize that everything that is good for you comes from God, then you will understand His will for you. Find your joy in God's grace, then He will speak love and comfort to you all the time.

5. Through your current situations. You may not hear the Lord during your time of struggle or your time of joy. You are in your current situation either as a result of your own doing or because God wants you there. If you are at rock bottom, then that's when the Lord will be there. When you are at wit's end, you'll find that God lives there. And when you are blessed beyond measure, the Lord is there, too, wanting to hear praise from you. "Every good gift and every perfect gift is from above, coming down from the Father of lights, with whom there is no variation or shadow due to change" (James 1:17).

Cade had not seen his journal for two years. The fact that it fell out from his car when he needed to hear from the Lord was not a coincidence. He was frustrated and irritated because he felt the Lord did not care about him and what he was going through. But it fell out to exactly what he needed to see. And it was in his own writing. God's timing is perfect. He will speak to you in His way. Be patient and be quiet. You'll hear from Him.

Chapter 16

GOD IS ALL YOU NEED

Trent Taylor
Wide Receiver / Punt Returner

But he said to me, "My grace is sufficient for you, for my power is made perfect in weakness." Therefore I will boast all the more gladly of my weaknesses, so that the power of Christ may rest upon me.

—2 Corinthians 12:9

When a punt returner goes back to catch the ball, he is aware of the danger that awaits him. The ball is kicked high into the air and usually sails about fifty-five yards down the field. The lone player attempts to catch the ball while sprinting players are going at full force to keep the punt returner from going very far once he hauls in the football. For a few moments, the returner is an open target and completely helpless to the defenders.

According to an article written in May 2022 by ESPN staff writer Kevin Seifert, "Special teams plays account for 30 percent of all ACL tears and 29 percent of muscle injuries to lower extremities." Trent knows the dangers of being a punt returner but also claims the protection of his Lord and Savior.

"I keep the mindset that Jesus Christ is enough for me all the time," he said. "Jesus is the only thing I need. Playing in the NFL is a dream come true and it's cool and all, but I don't need to be successful to have value."

The personal relationship Trent found in the Lord is everything in his life. He does not feel helpless but knows he is an open target by the devil.

"I grew up in church and always went to church," he said. "My parents taught me the Bible and how to live. I just think you see so many people get lost in the world. Coming to the NFL means you are at the top and can play at an elite level. We all want to be here, but there are still so many guys in this league who are so empty inside and have empty lives looking for things. They are looking for more and more because they don't have that relationship with Jesus. They buy anything that they can get their hands on because it makes them feel special for a few hours."

He said there are a lot of players who try to find happiness in the millions of dollars they make or the fans who scream their names and try to get autographs. But that does not bring lasting joy or happiness.

"I see some guys get lost in this crazy world," he said. "They are chasing the glamour or the fanfare or the limelight, but that only lasts a little while. Chasing material things doesn't last. But my relationship with Jesus Christ is worth more than all the money I can make."

He is grateful for his ability to play at the highest level on the football field and doesn't take that for granted. But he is also thankful that he can prioritize what really matters in life.

"One day I won't be on the football field," he said. "But I know that God will always be there for me and provide for me. I just know that."

The LORD is my shepherd; I shall not want. He makes me lie down in green pastures. He leads me beside still waters. He restores my soul. He leads me in paths of righteousness for his name's sake. Even though I walk through the valley of the shadow of death, I will fear no evil, for you are with me; your rod and your staff, they comfort me. You prepare a table before me in the presence of my enemies; you anoint my head with oil; my cup overflows. Surely goodness and mercy shall follow me all the days of my life, and I shall dwell in the house of the LORD forever.

—Psalm 23

4th and Goal

Life comes at you hard and without mercy or regard to your situations. It's just like Trent trying to catch a punt when the other team is barreling down on him. Trent's eyes are on the ball fluttering toward him in the air, while the defense is focused on him. Does that sound familiar to you? Are you the one with your eyes on something important and the devil is coming at you full steam? This is life. You know that just as soon as you field the ball, there will be two or three players ready to pounce on you and hit you without you seeing them come. You can hear the rumble of the footsteps, but you know that if you take your eyes off the ball, it could have disastrous consequences.

Touchdown

To stay focused on God's blessings and plans for your life amid the chaos sounds simple. Right? It should be. But you are human and have emotions and feelings. Life never stops. It comes barreling at you at times in waves and has no regard or recognition for your current situation. But you still have to catch the ball. Here are some ways to catch the ball in the middle of chaos.

1. Praise. Thank God for your blessings and for your faith. That might sound crazy to do, but when you acknowledge the Lord for all things, you will find strength. Ask and expect a miracle. But also accept His plan and look for the good in all situations because He is good all the time. "My mouth will tell of your righteous acts, of your deeds of salvation all the day, for their number is past my knowledge" (Psalm 71:15).
2. Volunteer. When you give the most valuable thing you have—your time—to a worthy cause, then you will be blessed in many ways. This allows you to put things into proper perspective. You may give comfort to a person who does not have a home or bed to sleep in at night. You might clothe a person who cannot afford a coat to stay warm. Or you might feed someone who doesn't know where their next meal will come from. These are

real problems, too, and they should not diminish your circumstances. When you lend a hand, you will be the recipient of God's blessings. "Whoever is generous to the poor lends to the LORD, and he will repay him for his deed" (Proverbs 19:17).

3. Talk. When life is coming at you hard, it's OK to talk to a pastor or another professional about it. Years ago, this was frowned upon but not anymore. The mind is a playground for the devil, and he knows this. If he can cause you to doubt and put awful images in your mind for a few moments, then he will. There is nothing wrong with seeking Christian counselors, pastors, or friends to bounce things off of. It should be a safe environment where the devil feels nervous.

4. Read. Read not only the Bible but also inspirational devotionals and books to feed your soul. Your mind needs strength just as football players need to go to the weight room all the time. Feed your brain with positive and inspirational items. "But he answered, 'It is written, "Man shall not live by bread alone, but by every word that comes from the mouth of God."'" (Matthew 4:4).

5. Attend. Go to church on a regular basis and also look for other events in your area. You can attend a Bible study, a Christian concert, or a local production to help you get away for a few. "But if we walk in the light, as he is in the light, we have fellowship with one another, and the blood of Jesus his Son cleanses us from all sin" (1 John 1:7).

Trent has the right idea because his focus is on the Lord. No matter what happens in his life, he knows God will take care of him. Life and circumstances might not go the way he intended or thought, but he accepts the will of the Father. He also knows that in the right time and place, he will find the riches of his rewards from the Lord.

Chapter 17

GOD'S LOVE FOR YOU IS AMAZING

Tycen Anderson
Safety

Do not be conformed to this world, but be transformed by the renewal of your mind, that by testing you may discern what is the will of God, what is good and acceptable and perfect.
—Romans 12:2

Some goals are so high they appear to be out of reach for some. You were probably encouraged to have dreams and expectations as a kid. Shoot for the moon and you'll hit some stars, right? Does that sound familiar?

Dreams do come true. Just ask Tycen.

His dream was to make it to the National Football League. That's a big order to fill, especially since there are about 1.1 million high school football players in the United States. And from those players, about 71,000 (6.5 percent) will go on to play football at the college level.

Then, out of those 71,000 athletes who make it to college, 1.2 percent will go on to play on Sundays at the highest level.

"It was always my dream to play in the NFL," Tycen said. "Ever since I was a kid, I had that dream and goal. And now, to be here to play football in my home state of Ohio is just amazing. I never lost sight of my dream."

Tycen was selected by the Cincinnati Bengals in the fifth round of the 2022 NFL Draft. He enjoyed a fantastic college career at Toledo and started all fourteen games as a freshman. In that first season, Tycen had thirty tackles and broke up four passes. He made a name for himself, and scouts caught wind of his talents.

The next season, which was shortened to six games because of COVID-19, he was named second-team All-MAC (Mid-American Conference).

In his final season at Toledo, he recorded forty-four tackles at safety and was first-team All-MAC. But still, he knew the odds of making it to the NFL were slim but within reach.

"Being a football player in Ohio and then being drafted by the Bengals was an incredible feeling and moment in my life," Tycen added. "It's been a struggle to get here. I've been through a lot of ups and downs. But it's such a blessing because I know God has had His hand in this for it to happen. For me to be here is because of God's love for me. He knew what I wanted and how hard I worked and made a way."

When Tycen learned that he was selected to go to the next level, he realized that all the hard work was rewarded. He never gave up and worked hard toward his goal.

"My message to anyone who is a believer in Christ—or even if you're not—just know that He loves you and wants the very best for you," he added. "God will love you on the good days and on the bad ones. He does that for me every day. I just learn from the Word of God and put myself around people who encourage me. That makes a big difference and helps you in your walk."

To stay in the NFL, Tycen knows he must work harder than he did to get there. He is grateful to be in the locker room and knows it will not last forever.

"I got here," he said. "And my plan is to stay here and play. I hope that's what God wants for me. But if it's not, I'll be thankful for the time I had and look for the next blessing."

Keep yourselves in the love of God, waiting for the mercy of our Lord Jesus Christ that leads to eternal life.

—Jude 21

4th and Goal

What are your dreams? What do you hope to accomplish? Do you want to make the first string on the football team? Do you want to help your team win the conference championship? Or perhaps your goal is to be promoted to a senior-level position with your company? Maybe you want to start your own business. Or your dream might be to join the military or become a law enforcement officer. You may have a desire to be a missionary or help those in need.

Touchdown

While you are waiting on God's timing in your life, there are many things you can do to prepare and pass the time. You can continue to work hard toward your goal. You can stay in good physical condition by exercising and keep your mind sharp by reading. But what else can you do? Did you ever consider helping others? You know that God loves you. But here are some ways you can show love toward others while you wait.

1. Be an encouragement to others. While you wait for that special moment, lift others up around you. You don't need to discuss your situation, but instead focus on those around you. Take an interest in their lives and help them on their journey. Send out encouraging text messages or cards. Kind words will go a long way. "I appeal to you, brothers, by the name of our Lord Jesus Christ, that all of you agree, and that there be no divisions among you, but that you be united in the same mind and the same judgment" (1 Corinthians 1:10).
2. Give a lift. If you know someone who needs a ride to church or to work, reach out and offer to help. Be cautious about picking up strangers but offer up to friends or colleagues.
3. Share or cook a meal. Offer your home for a get-together and provide or make a meal for your guests. When you provide a meal and good company, you show love and hospitality. Ask nothing in return and be careful not to attract a clique.
4. Be a prayer. One of the best ways to show love is to pray with people. If you are in a church service and some respond and go to the altar to seek God, go with them and be a support and intercessor. When you pray with someone, you create a common bond, and you

send the message that you are there for the person. Love them. "First of all, then, I urge that supplications, prayers, intercessions, and thanksgivings be made for all people, for kings and all who are in high positions, that we may lead a peaceful and quiet life, godly and dignified in every way" (1 Timothy 2:1–2).

5. Get involved. This can be in local government, sports, or civic groups. Don't do this for personal gain but to be of service and to make a difference. There are many areas where you can get involved. It's limitless. Find an area that you relate to and jump in. "And let us not grow weary of doing good, for in due season we will reap, if we do not give up" (Galatians 6:9).

When you show love to others while you wait, you put yourself in position to be blessed by the Lord. That should never be the reason you do it, but it's definitely a benefit. Tycen worked hard and reaped the benefits of his work and God's love. He knew the Lord wanted the best for him. The Lord wants the best for you too. But He also wants to see you show love for others.

Chapter 18

WHO DO YOU PLAY FOR?

Jaylen Waddle
Wide Receiver

But those who trust in the L<small>ORD</small> will find new strength. They will soar high on wings like eagles. They will run and not grow weary. They will walk and not faint.
—Isaiah 40:31 NLT

When this was written, Jaylen's Twitter profile was very clear when it came to letting everyone know how he feels about the Lord Jesus Christ. "In Jesus Name I Play" is what followers see. That is as direct as you can get. There is no beating around the bush. Jaylen loves the Lord. The Alabama Crimson Tide product said he attributes his faith to his mother.

"I grew up in church, and my mom was a big believer in the Lord," he said. "I just stayed with that because she said that I played for Jesus and in His name. I just kept that and believed that too. It's just who I am and who I play for."

In the 2021 NFL Draft, the Miami Dolphins snatched up the wide receiver in the first round on the sixth overall pick. He was excited and honored to be the first selection by the Dolphins because he said he had faced some challenges the year before at Alabama.

"I got banged up a lot my last year in college," he said. "It was a time where I needed to rely on my faith and prayer because it got really tough."

But he made it through and made it to the NFL. During the week-12 game against the Carolina Panthers, Jaylen racked up 137 yards receiving and helped the Dolphins win 33–10. Four weeks later he broke Anquan Boldin's record of 101 season receptions when he pulled down a total of 104 catches to set a new NFL rookie record for most receptions. He definitely made an impact in his first season in the league.

The next year, he picked up right where he left off. In the second game of the young season, Jaylen grabbed eleven catches for 171 yards and two touchdowns in a 42–38 win over Baltimore. He set another NFL record on Christmas Day when he caught an eighty-four-yard touchdown, which established the longest scoring play in the NFL on Christmas.

He earned a solid reputation as a legitimate threat to score on any play. And he also caught the eyes of the fans each time he scored. Jaylen established "The Waddle" celebration every time he scored a touchdown, obviously inspired by his last name. He will waddle like a duck or penguin in the end zone to celebrate a TD. It's cute to his fans and teammates. But that's not what he wants to be remembered for.

"I don't want to be remembered just for making big plays on Sunday," he said. "It's fun catching touchdowns and stuff like that—celebrating with my teammates—but I want to get into the community and make a big difference. I didn't really have a role model growing up, and so for me, I want to be one for someone else. I want to lead the way and inspire young people. I want them to see Jesus in me."

> *I pray that God, the source of hope, will fill you completely with joy and peace because you trust in him. Then you will overflow with confident hope through the power of the Holy Spirit.*
>
> —Romans 15:13 NLT

4th and Goal

You will have several opportunities to create an image or memory for those in your circle. If you mess up, you might still have time to set the record straight. Life happens and people make mistakes. A bad choice should never define who you are. If you are willing to make the changes then hopefully those important to you will notice. Maybe you have an issue with a temper or foul language. Perhaps you are known for being dishonest when it comes to your work ethic. Or perhaps you just want to be like Jaylen and be a positive role model.

Touchdown

You want to be remembered for the good things you do and not the bad stuff. That's human. But what about that negative habit you have? Or that bad reputation? Once you give those over to the Lord, He will forgive you and help you be the person you wish to be. Here are some suggestions to help you in your journey to be the best person possible.

1. Be a person who prays. Talk with the Lord on a regular basis. Don't pray to obtain the applause and approval of others but do it because He is your Father. Prayer brings you closer to the Lord. Prayer makes a difference and will encourage you to listen and will invite you to be patient in your walk. Christ is not a wishing well. He wants to hear from you . . . and not just when you are in a jam. Communication is the key to any relationship. This includes your Christian walk. "So let us come boldly to the throne of our gracious God. There we will receive his mercy, and we will find grace to help us when we need it most" (Hebrews 4:16 NLT).
2. Be a person who is honest. You can be honest and true ninety-nine times, but people will remember that one time you weren't. That's not fair, but that is how humanity works. Life is not fair. Your coworkers or the community you run with will notice the few times you might be less than honest. When you look back throughout history, you can see that the hardest part of life is defending a lie. It's not worth it. Be the person others can turn to for the truth. Let them see God in you. "Then you will understand what is right, just, and fair, and you will find the right way to go" (Proverbs 2:9 NLT).
3. Be a person who does good. Do good deeds for yourself and for those who receive your generosity. It doesn't matter if your buddies see you do good. That doesn't

matter because you are not doing good for them. Do good because God calls you to be a servant. It molds your character and if your kids or spouse notice your actions, then that's a big bonus.
4. Be a person who makes a positive difference. This is not a hard assignment. Open doors for people. Smile. Thank those who help you. Allow drivers in a crowded lane to slip in front of you. Help a waiter clean up after you. Get involved with civic organizations and be there for your family.
5. Be a person who is happy. When the Lord takes over your heart, you can tackle each day with a positive attitude. You may have circumstances in your life that may not be pleasant, but you can have peace and joy in your heart as you face them. "Yes, the LORD has done amazing things for us! What joy!" (Psalm 126:3 NLT).

Jaylen is known in the NFL as an effective receiver who can score TDs and help his team win. He is also known as a player who likes to celebrate his accomplishments on the field. But that is what he does for a living. He knows it's more important for him to be regarded as a positive role model. What about you?

Chapter 19

THINK ABOUT THE POSITIVES

Jalen Ramsey
All-Pro Cornerback

And he answered, "You shall love the Lord your God with all your heart and with all your soul and with all your strength and with all your mind, and your neighbor as yourself."
—Luke 10:27

If you watch the news on a regular basis, you are exposed to constant negativity. There isn't much hope out there according to the media. Most of the time, all you will be exposed to is doom and gloom.

From bizarre crime waves to politics, the world can be a dreary place to live. With the onslaught of bleak and cynical happenings posted on social media and on the daily news, it's no coincidence that discouragement and depression run rampant in society. Uplifting news is rare today. But it makes a big difference.

Everyday struggles are common and a part of life. No one enjoys a bed of roses twenty-four hours a day. But if you follow Christ, you know that there is a balm of Gilead to help soothe your pain.

"There are struggles in life every day," Jalen said. "And there will always be struggles. Ain't no day that's easy. They don't exist. But I know that, through my Lord and Savior Jesus Christ, anything is possible. I know that He takes care of me, and I always have hope because of that."

The world and the devil want you to be bombarded with negative thoughts. They want you to be consumed with negativity. There are many disasters and events that invite heartache. But extended bouts of negativity can result in serious health problems. According to a study from the Mayo Clinic, negativity sends our body into stress or "fight-or-flight" mode. God designed your body to deal with stress by releasing cortisol into the bloodstream, which makes you more alert and able to focus.

But extended amounts of doom and gloom slows digestion and decreases the immune system's ability to fight inflammation. There are some common side effects from having a negative mindset. These include headaches, chest pain, fatigue, upset stomach, insomnia, anxiety, depression, overeating, undereating, and moodiness.

That doesn't sound fun at all.

But Jalen has the attitude to let the Master take on his battles.

"I have the promises He gave me," he said. "I know I have His grace and mercy upon me. I know I am favored because I am a child of God. I am blessed and those things I keep in mind, especially during struggles. I don't think about the negativity or negative thoughts. I think about the positives that can come out of every situation. Even if it might be a bad moment or a bad situation, I know that God is bringing me through it for a specific reason. That is how I look at it. That's the way I think about everything. He's been faithful to me and has made miracles happen in my life."

Having the glory of God, its radiance like a most rare jewel, like a jasper, clear as crystal.
—Revelation 21:11

4th and Goal

Who enjoys being around people who are always negative? Those who wallow in self-pity and negativity want to pull you down in the sewer with them. It's easier to complain and seek validation than to be positive and look for ways to make a situation better. Being negative is almost like having an addiction. Those who constantly complain do it because they have fallen into the habit. The devil has been successful in painting a pessimistic picture of rejection and hopelessness.

Touchdown

Don't fall into the pigpen of negativity and become a defeatist. If you look for the silver lining in events, you will be better off in the long run. This doesn't mean you look the other way in difficult situations or put your head in the sand and ignore circumstances. It means you know that God will take care of you no matter what happens. And there are great benefits to having a positive attitude. It will increase your lifespan, lower your stress levels, boost your immune system to fight off illness, reduce your risk of death from cancer and death from respiratory conditions. It will also provide you with better coping skills during tense moments and will encourage you to laugh and smile more. Here are some steps to take if you want to have a positive mindset as a Christian.

1. Deepen your relationship with the Lord. This sounds basic but the best way to do this is to dive into the Word of God and pray more often. Look into meaningful devotions and spend more time with the intention of growing your relationship. You will get out of what you put into the relationship. "And we know that for those who love God all things work together for good, for those who are called according to his purpose" (Romans 8:28).
2. Take inventory on a regular basis. Write an inventory of your actions regularly. Examine how your behavior aligns with the Lord's directions for your life. Write down how you react to stress or manage anger and how you treat your loved ones and family members. Show self-compassion and be patient with yourself. But be honest. You cannot improve if you lie to yourself. The best way to address it is to notice it and write it down for analysis.
3. Let go. Toss out anger and resentment. When you throw out anger and negative emotions, you will be happier and content. This doesn't mean to let others

walk over you with words or actions, but it means that you can only control your thoughts and not how others treat you. "See to it that no one fails to obtain the grace of God; that no 'root of bitterness' springs up and causes trouble, and by it many become defiled" (Hebrews 12:15).

4. Help others. Doing random acts of kindness can help you grow in spirit. Donate your time to a worthy cause or help prepare a meal for a family in need. Help others without expecting gratitude or applause.
5. Connect with others. Learning to feel connected with other people can make you more resilient. It is also part of God's plan; we are meant to live within a community of people. Take time to listen to others and be receptive to their ideas. When you are a good listener, you become a better friend. "Therefore encourage one another and build one another up, just as you are doing" (1 Thessalonians 5:11).

Jalen knows that if he depends on the Lord to take care of him, he has no reason to be negative. You can have the same outlook and have inner peace and happiness. You are a child of God and that is reason enough to smile through it all.

Chapter 20

GOD WILL PROVIDE A SAFE LANDING

Jordan Kunaszyk
Linebacker

Continue steadfastly in prayer, being watchful in it with thanksgiving. At the same time, pray also for us, that God may open to us a door for the word, to declare the mystery of Christ, on account of which I am in prison—that I may make it clear, which is how I ought to speak. Walk in wisdom toward outsiders, making the best use of the time. Let your speech always be gracious, seasoned with salt, so that you may know how you ought to answer each person.
—Colossians 4:2–6

When you finally decide to follow the Lord on the Christian journey, that will be the best day and decision ever. No one has ever said that accepting God's offer of salvation was a mistake. You will have made the choice to trust in the Savior and have life everlasting. Your sins will be thrown away forever and will not be remembered anymore by the Lord.

There is no downside or reason to regret the decision to be saved. You will have peace of mind and joy in your heart. But this doesn't mean life will be easy.

"A lot of today's Christianity believes that if you come to Jesus then He will give you a good life and it will be rainbows and butterflies," Jordan said. "But Scripture says the opposite. It tells us that we will be persecuted, and we are going to go through suffering. But it also says we can take courage because He has overcome the world; it's not that Christianity doesn't provide a safe flight, but it does provide a safe landing."

When you focus on the destination instead of the bumps along the journey, it will provide incentive to keep going. That attitude is essential when trials and troubles come into your life.

"Just knowing that my eternity will be with Jesus is enough," Jordan added. "And it says in Revelation that in the new heavens and new earth, there will be no more weeping and no more pain and no more mourning and sadness or suffering because old things have passed away. So just knowing that I will get to see my Creator and Savior face-to-face and be with Him eternally and all I need to do is just continue to take up my cross daily and just walk by faith and not by sight and love Him with all my heart and soul and strength and love my neighbor as myself."

Jordan's description is spot-on, and his attitude is almost perfect. The key is to put those words into actions.

"Just His grace is amazing and that I don't have to do anything to earn it and I don't deserve it," Jordan said. "But He graciously gave it all. I just accept it and praise Him for the wonderful gifts and for salvation."

For through the law I died to the law, so that I might live to God. I have been crucified with Christ. It is no longer I who live, but Christ who lives in me. And the life I now live in the flesh I live by faith in the Son of God, who loved me and gave himself for me. I do not nullify the grace of God, for if righteousness were through the law, then Christ died for no purpose.
—Galatians 2:19–21

4th and Goal

When everything goes your way, it's easy to thank God for your blessings. Jordan gives the Lord credit but not because he plays in the NFL. He's had his share of uncertainty and discouragement. Over the years, he has been released or signed to a practice team instead of the actual team. However, his focus is not on football but on the Father. God is with you in the good and bad times. But you may not realize that when life has sacked you and forced you to turn the ball over.

Touchdown

Always be prepared for an all-out blitz from the devil. He will disguise the defensive formation to try to catch you off guard. Just when you are ready to cross the goal line, he will cause a distraction to entice you to jump offsides or commit a flagrant penalty. When you face persecution, how will you react? Will you forget the price the Lord paid, or will you rise to the occasion and take a stand for Christ? You may be going through rejection, grief, loss, or discouragement. Throughout your challenges, remember that God will provide. He took care of the children of Israel, Job, David, Shadrach, Meshach, and Abednego. Here are some things to consider why you should always be thankful for His mercy, salvation, and promise to take care of you.

1. He will comfort you. You will experience loss. There will be the death of a loved one. You may lose your job or even your home or friends. During this time, you might be discouraged and tempted by the devil to give up. But remember that God's faithfulness will carry you through the rough parts and deliver you to victory. His gift of comfort is bigger than adversity. Just because you are a believer, you are not free from problems. But you will have a safe landing. "So also you have sorrow now, but I will see you again, and your hearts will rejoice, and no one will take your joy from you" (John 16:22).
2. He will provide strength. This does not mean the kind of strength where you can pick up a car but rather the spiritual strength to get through. There will be times when life weighs heavy on you or kicks you when you are down. God's power will strengthen you at the right time and for the right cause. God will allow you to reach a point where you depend on Him instead of you. God's grace and love *is* power. "The LORD is my strength and my song, and he has become my salvation; this is my God, and I will praise him, my father's God, and I will exalt him" (Exodus 15:2).
3. He will support you. The Lord will do this through your church community or solid friends. He will send

people into your life to talk and pray with you. This community could be friends, small groups, a Bible study, or an online group. God uses and speaks through different people who can encourage you. But keep in mind that God is the ultimate source of wisdom and support. Seek His will via prayer and fasting. Christ is always faithful.

4. He will encourage you. He will do this through Scripture. Dig into the Word of God and find the promises He made to you. He loves you. These words will uplift and encourage you at the right time. If you are overwhelmed, flip to Philippians 4:13 where the Word tells you that you can do all things through Christ who gives you strength. "May the God of hope fill you with all joy and peace in believing, so that by the power of the Holy Spirit you may abound in hope" (Romans 15:13).

5. He will remind you of His love. When life or circumstances don't make sense, just remember that He loves you so much that He sent Jesus to the cross to die for you so you can have life everlasting. That is how much God loves you. "For God so loved the world, that he gave his only Son, that whoever believes in him should not perish but have eternal life" (John 3:16).

Jordan said that Christians are not guaranteed rainbows and butterflies. But you, through the blood of Christ, can enjoy the benefits of the heavenly Father. The landing He provides will be the smoothest one of all time.

Chapter 21

YOU MATTER SO MUCH TO THE LORD

Hayden Hurst
Tight End

Come to me, all who labor and are heavy laden, and I will give you rest.
—Matthew 11:28

Never take happiness for granted. Never take your life for granted.

You may be the individual everyone loves to be around. Maybe you are the life of the party. You draw people to you like a magnet. Others enjoy your company and believe you have it all together.

But deep down, you are fighting demons who want to see you give up and die.

Hayden knows all about this.

The 6-4, 250-pounder from Jacksonville, Florida, was drafted to play professional baseball by the Pittsburgh Pirates in 2012. He turned down an athletic scholarship at Florida State to pursue a professional pitching career.

The mound was not friendly to Hayden, who decided to walk on and play college football at South Carolina two years later.

But in January 2016, it all came crashing down. The soon-to-be twenty-fifth pick in the first round of the 2018 NFL Draft woke up in a hospital after a failed suicide attempt. He cut his wrist, and a friend found him bleeding to death in his apartment, unconscious, and called for help.

"I lived a crazy life for a long time," he said. "But I had my suicide attempt when I was only twenty-two. For whatever reason, God looked down and gave me a second chance. I want to do the best I can to make the most of it and help my family.

"Football is fabulous, but a solid foundation is more incredible. Being on the field is pretty great and cool, but being able to have an impact and help people save some lives is awesome too."

When he was playing baseball, he developed a case of the yips—wrist spasms—on the mound and suffered from anxiety and depression. The once-promising Pittsburgh pitcher couldn't find the strike zone. In fact, he had no control of the baseball, and he was unpredictable on the mound. He tried to fix it with cocaine or anything else he could find. But that did not work. Getting high and stoned only made things worse.

"When you are in that headspace and you are depressed, you have suicidal ideas and hear all kinds of voices telling you that you don't matter and that you are worthless," Hayden added. "It's very hard to get out of that tough process. It just consumes you. For me, I leaned on drugs and alcohol and that exacerbated it more and made it worse. I had no idea and was trying to find anything to help me. I was in a vicious cycle spinning around and around."

Hayden hit rock bottom and ended up on his back in a hospital. He was handcuffed to the bed and on suicide watch for seventy-two hours, he said. That was when Christ appeared to Hayden. Amid all the chaos, Jesus was right on time.

Hayden appeared to have it all to some. He was a promising athlete with an addictive personality, but no one saw the signs that he wanted to end his life.

"It's always that happiest person in the room who suffers quietly when they're alone, and no one suspects at all," he said. "People who end up taking their life put on a good front. It runs in my family."

His uncle was a happy-go-lucky guy but took his own life.

"It's usually those who you least suspect or expect to do this," Hayden said. "You never know what someone is going through. Everyone has their own demons to fight and it's best to let God fight them. I found that out after I tried to kill myself."

Now, he makes a point to treat everyone the way he wants to be treated.

"It's simple to do, but a lot of people find that hard to do," he said. "Just treat people nice and be kind. It sounds simple, but it is really that easy. Just smile and be kind."

> *The salvation of the righteous is from the LORD; he is their stronghold in the time of trouble.*
>
> —Psalm 37:39

4th and Goal

Do you go through times when you are discouraged, and no one is aware? Are you the life of the party? Do people think you have it all going for you but deep down you struggle to be happy? Have you allowed the devil to put terrible thoughts in your head about taking your life? Are you afraid to let others know because you are afraid of what church leaders or others in the congregation might think? These are a lot of tough questions that need to be asked. Do you matter? Does God really love you?

Touchdown

Of course you matter. You are important and have value, no matter what your enemies want you to believe. Depression and anxiety and discouragement are real. These symptoms and conditions can be difficult to admit to, but take the stand or listen to your loved ones who may notice. It's OK. The condition is serious and needs attention from professionals, and most of all, from the Lord. He cares for you. There are many things that might contribute to depression. The death of a loved one. A job loss. A bad relationship. Abuse from someone you trust. Addiction. Fear of failure or rejection or ridicule. The list can go on and on. Whatever the reason, it needs to be addressed. Here are some ways to cling to the Lord in your time of need.

1. Call for help. If you are thinking about ending your life, call the 988 Suicide & Crisis Lifeline. You can call or text 988 any time, day or night, and receive a response.

Then call your pastor or a close friend who can help. Realize your need for Christ. If you are a Christian, pray and dive into the Word of God. He wants the best for you. "In your righteousness deliver me and rescue me; incline your ear to me, and save me!" (Psalm 71:2).

2. Praise. Do this in the quiet of your home if you must. When you give glory to the Master, even when you hurt, the Lord will lift you up and encourage you. "Then they cried to the LORD in their trouble, and he delivered them from their distress" (Psalm 107:28).
3. Help others. This is a great way to get your mind off your problems. Be an inspiration for someone who is at their lowest point. When you can encourage someone who struggles, you are the one who is helped even more. "In my distress I called upon the LORD; to my God I cried for help. From his temple he heard my voice, and my cry to him reached his ears" (Psalm 18:6).
4. Listen to inspirational music. Allow God to speak to you through music. This can help you through some dark times. You can find a song that relates to your situation and identify with it. Then you can find the strength to keep going. Discover your personal anthem.
5. Journal. This is one of the best ways to cope. Put your thoughts down in writing and cry out to God with your pen or with your fingers on your computer. Get off social media and keep your journal private. Be specific in what you write and put down what you want to see happen. This gives you time to calm down and examine the situation. You can put down your prayers and hopes. David did this all throughout the Psalms.

This can be therapeutic in so many ways. "The Lord will rescue me from every evil deed and bring me safely into his heavenly kingdom. To him be the glory forever and ever. Amen" (2 Timothy 4:18).

Depression and discouragement for a Christian can be a scary walk that may be filled with judgment by those who don't understand. The point here is not to get to the dark place where you do what Hayden did—he tried to kill himself. God does not want that, nor will He honor that choice. Live for Christ and find the peace and joy He offers at no charge. You matter.

Chapter 22

FOCUS

Corey Bojorquez
Punter

For those who live according to the flesh set their minds on the things of the flesh, but those who live according to the Spirit set their minds on the things of the Spirit.
—Romans 8:5

Corey is an exceptional punter. On October 17, 2021, he booted the pigskin eighty-two yards in the third quarter for the Green Bay Packers, who eventually won the game 24–14 over the Chicago Bears. That amazing punt was a career long kick for the undrafted New Mexico product.

It's hard to believe, but the eighty-two yarder was not the longest punt in NFL history, but it was the longest that season. The longest one came on September 21, 1969, when New York Jets punter Steve O'Neal blasted a ninety-eight-yard punt in a game against the Denver Broncos. That's an incredible record that may never be broken.

In week 17 of the 2022 season, Corey played for the Cleveland Browns and booted two punts inside the Washington Commanders' twenty-yard line and had a sixty-four yarder as well to help the Browns win 24–10 and earn him the AFC Special Teams Player of the Week.

To be an effective punter in the NFL takes an extraordinary amount of focus. He has, on average, about 1.2 seconds to get the ball in the air and off his foot before defenders get to him. When the football is snapped to the kicker, it takes about 1.9 to 1.95 seconds to get to him. He must catch the snap and punt the ball downfield with about nine to ten players coming after him, all while he is exposed to the rush and defenseless.

It looks easy, but it is a tough job to fill. A good punt can put the defense in a solid position while a shanked kick can cost field position and give the offense a short trip to the end zone.

Corey works hard to be an effective punter, but he also has his life in perspective. "My faith in God helps me to keep things in the right order," he said. "It keeps you focused on the most important things in life—family, love, trust, and hope."

But at one time, Christ was not the center of his life.

"I grew up with religion, but it wasn't the most important thing in my life at the time," he added. "When I met my wife in college, that was big for me. She got me going to church more and more and wanted that for me and for us. She wanted me to get to know God closer and have a relationship with Him. I appreciated her for that."

Once Corey put his focus on the Master, life came into perspective. Life was not perfect, but he had peace and happiness in his heart.

"Now, Christ is the focal point in my life and not football," he said. "Life is about God. I try to grow every day and help her too. We just had a daughter, and we just want to raise her to know the Lord too. Jesus Christ sacrificed His life and is everything to us. We want her to be raised in church and read the Bible, and we all want to pray together. That's the focal point."

> *There is therefore now no condemnation for those who are in Christ Jesus.*
> —Romans 8:1

4th and Goal

The world is filled with distractions. Some are good while some can lead you astray. Whatever takes your full attention away to something else is a distraction. Positive distractions might include taking a walk, singing, creating art, doodling, or writing. Those can be considered habits as well. Some negative distractions may be loud music while you're trying to sleep or annoying noises if you are reading or praying. If something attracts your attention from what you are trying to focus on, then it's a distraction.

Touchdown

It is easy to get wrapped up in life to the point where certain things can consume you. There is nothing wrong with a good book or a sports devotional, but you can also read God's letter to you. There is nothing wrong with a round of golf with buddies, but it should not interfere with going to church or revival services. Time off is needed, but it should never take away from Christ. Work can also pull you all over and in many directions. But it should not be your God. Some emails and text messages can wait until your kids go to bed. Here are some ways to keep focused on what matters.

1. Good routines. Get in the habit of reading your Bible and devotions at the same time each day. You know when Monday Night Football is and you won't miss that. Or you may have to sit in on conference calls at the same time each day. Put God on your schedule and make it a good habit and follow it up with prayer. Don't whiz through it and act like you are doing God a favor. Put in the time and make it work, just like you do if you go to the gym. "'All things are lawful for me,' but not all things are helpful. 'All things are lawful for me,' but I will not be dominated by anything" (1 Corinthians 6:12).
2. Don't overextend yourself. Learn the power or the little two-letter word *no*. Life can come at you fast, and there is a lot to do. You can be involved at church and in small groups, your kids' extracurricular activities, work, a social life, civic organizations, and so on. Before you know it, you cannot make time for God or church. If something prevents you from spending time with the Lord or His house, then it is a distraction and needs to be adjusted or eliminated.
3. Set time aside. In the frenzy of the day, just a few minutes of prayer or reflection can help give you a boost.

Take a few moments to send a positive text to your spouse or a friend who may be discouraged. Set time aside for others and not for you. This will keep you focused. "You desire and do not have, so you murder. You covet and cannot obtain, so you fight and quarrel. You do not have, because you do not ask" (James 4:2).

4. Be active. You might think this contradicts the second point, but it does not. If you sit around and are bored, then it's easy to become lazy, and that is a distraction. You will find yourself on the couch with a bag of chips watching TV or scrolling on your phone. That's a bad idea. Life doesn't have to be a blur, but it also doesn't need to feel like it's the seventh overtime. Be active in your kids' lives without being in control. Join a civic group and be charitable or take up a fun hobby.

5. Be healthy. Eat a healthy diet and exercise and get the right amount of rest. If you feel bad, go see your doctor. The point is to take care of yourself spiritually, mentally, and physically. When you feel better, you can focus better. "Beloved, I pray that all may go well with you and that you may be in good health, as it goes well with your soul" (3 John 2).

Your work is important and so is your family or friends. You may think you can juggle seven balls, but they will overtake you if you take your eyes off them. It will happen. You will lose focus because you have too much going on. Step back and stay focused and fixed on the Lord and life will be balanced and more fun.

Chapter 23

GOD WANTS YOU ON HIS TEAM

Michael Thomas
Safety

As you come to him, a living stone rejected by men but in the sight of God chosen and precious.
—1 Peter 2:4

Not being wanted is a lousy feeling. Do you know of anyone who was always picked last on the middle school playground? Perhaps you were that one who was overlooked. Or maybe you were the person who overlooked others. In either case, it must stink to have a feeling of not being wanted.

Rejection is a powerful tool the devil has in his arsenal. And he knows how to entice and persuade people to use it to perfection. Rejection can send a person into emotional distress.

When Michael's collegiate football career was over at Stanford University, no NFL team drafted him. No squad showed enough confidence in him to pick him for their team.

He finally signed with the San Francisco 49ers as an undrafted free agent in 2012 and spent the first year on the practice squad. In December 2013, he inked a deal to be part of the Miami Dolphins. Two years later he made the first string and had thirteen starts. On December 20, he collected eleven tackles against San Diego and finished the season with eighty-five tackles.

In week 13, 2017, he suffered a knee injury after playing in thirteen games. The next year, he signed a two-year contract with the New York Giants. The 2018 season was his best as a pro. He had fifty-nine tackles, two interceptions, and a sack, and earned Pro Bowl honors.

Two seasons later, he landed in Houston but suffered a season-ending injury in week 10. But in October 2021, Michael landed on the Cincinnati Bengals practice squad and was elevated to the active roster the next month. A couple of months later, he played in the Super Bowl against the Los Angeles Rams. What a journey!

He has an incredible comeback story because when the season started, Michael did not have a team. He told the *Sports Spectrum* podcast that God gets all the glory.

"God's plans are far greater than ours, man. . . . I wasn't signed anywhere, but I wasn't stressing about it," Thomas said. "I knew God had a plan for me regardless of what that is, but I was very content and ready to transition if I needed to."

Michael used to carry his own load and rely on his ability rather than let God, and maybe that is why he bounced around the league.

"My faith grew first and the most through football," he added. "I was a rookie, and in my second year I put everything on me and thought that if I just gave it my all that everything would work out."

He went on the field and gave all he had.

"It still wasn't enough for the team," he said. "I was humbled by that and that was the first time I had to lean on something beyond me. I'm not strong enough, and that's when my faith grew."

Once Michael decided to let the Lord lead, things changed.

"I said, 'OK, Lord, I understand. Show me what I need to do,'" he said. "I can honestly say that each day I trust in Him and give every situation to Him. That's when I got the message that every single day, I must lean on Him, and I can go to work worry free every day."

Michael went from one extreme to the other—from experiencing rejection when no team wanted him to making an impact on a team that went to a Super Bowl. Only God can do that for you.

But he said to me, "My grace is sufficient for you, for my power is made perfect in weakness." Therefore I will boast all the more gladly of my weaknesses, so that the power of Christ may rest upon me.
—2 Corinthians 12:9

4th and Goal

Have you ever experienced rejection in your life? Maybe it was in a relationship or on the job or by family or so-called friends. The message sent by rejection is not well received. It can increase and invite anger, anxiety, depression, jealousy, and sadness. Rejection can reduce performance at the job site or in the classroom and can contribute to aggression and poor decision-making. Because of rejection, you can often look for acceptance in the wrong places. The devil can make alcohol, drugs, gambling, or sex look comforting.

Touchdown

People can be cruel when it comes to rejection. Some do not realize the damage rejection can do to you. And to be honest, some may not even care. Jesus Christ was rejected by the world and by man. This is not a comparison to your situation, but keep that in mind the next time it happens to you. Rejection is not fun and can have devastating effects if not handled in a biblical way. Here are some ways to handle moments when you are rejected.

1. Recognize and accept. Rejection is real and most of the time is caused by more than one person. The old saying is true: "hurt people hurt people." When someone lashes out or rejects you, it's because they may have been hurt, too, somewhere along the way. Don't try to justify or minimize the situation. Search your own heart and see if you had a part in the mess. "Search me, O God, and know my heart! Try me and know my thoughts! And see if there be any grievous way in me, and lead me in the way everlasting!" (Psalm 139:23–24).
2. Forgive all parties involved. Especially those who have rejected you. Forgive them. Pray for them and give them space. When the seed of bitterness is planted, it

grows fast. When you forgive, even if the other person does not, you have peace and joy in your heart. "Jesus said to him, 'I do not say to you seven times, but seventy-seven times'" (Matthew 18:22).

3. Show unconditional love. This might be a challenge to do, but it is necessary for spiritual growth. The easy way out is to ignore the person and don't give them another chance. But that is exactly what Satan wants. He desires division and separation. As a believer and follower of Christ, you are called to a higher standard. When you face rejection from family or friends, put on the love of God. Don't let them walk over you but pray for them and show love to the best of your ability.

4. Seek comfort. There are support groups that you might be able to relate to or a pastor or prayer partner to reach out to. There are no good sides to rejection. It hurts. But remember that Christ was also rejected by enemies and by those closest to Him. You are not alone. This doesn't make it any easier, but you can talk to the One who was rejected in prayer. "Take my yoke upon you, and learn from me, for I am gentle and lowly in heart, and you will find rest for your souls" (Matthew 11:29).

5. Find peace. It's available to you through the blood of Christ. Don't push or rush reconciliation. It will happen when the Lord sees fit. But pray and ask for patience while you wait. If you have been hurt and rejected, step back and let yourself heal. Allow the Lord to handle the moment. When it's out of your control, step back and watch God work. While you wait, ask the Lord to show you ways to grow as a Christian and a person.

Michael could have given up and gone down a new path when no team showed interest in him in the draft. Instead, he put his head down and plowed through. He leaned on his faith and trusted his ability. He experienced humility and used that to increase his dependence on God. He overcame, and you can too.

Chapter 24

JUST PRAY

Tee Higgins
Wide Receiver

Be anxious for nothing, but in everything by prayer and supplication, with thanksgiving, let your requests be made known to God; and the peace of God, which surpasses all understanding, will guard your hearts and minds through Christ Jesus.
—Philippians 4:6–7 NKJV

Prayer is powerful. It's the only act of communication by humans with our Holy God. Prayer energizes your heart as a believer through the power of the Spirit. Consistent prayer releases the power of God's blessings in your life and all situations. It should never be used as a last resort, but as your first option. And the best part about prayer is that He listens. No matter the circumstances or the moment, God is there. He is not a rescue plan, or a get-out-of-jail-free card. He is your heavenly Father and wants to hear from you.

Tee is a big advocate of prayer. He believes in an open line to Jesus Christ.

"My faith means everything to me. I pray when I get up in the morning," he said. "I thank God for another day. I pray when I walk into the building, and I pray in the locker room and when I walk onto the field. I pray before the game. I pray during the game, and I pray after the game and before I go to bed. I pray. I pray. I pray."

The second-round pick in the 2020 NFL Draft said he learned about prayer as a kid and makes it a part of his life today.

"I play through God," he added. "Without Him, I am nothing. He gives me strength and gives me this talent and ability. This is who I am. He has blessed me and wants me to be great. Great as a person, and great in this league and in my job. Everything I am or have today is because of Him."

Tee had a stressful childhood that came to a head when his mother was shot when he was just in kindergarten. He was called to the school office as a little boy where he found his sister crying. He was told his mom was shot in the head by her boyfriend.

"I just remember all those police cars and the ambulance," he said. "All I wanted to do was see my mom, but no one would let me. I just wanted to see her because I didn't know what was going on."

His mother struggled with drug addiction but has been clean and sober for several years.

"Whenever I'm having a bad day or having an issue I'm having, it just doesn't compare to what my mom went through," he said. "She overcame drugs, getting shot, and fighting addiction, and overcoming it all these years. If I ever have a problem, I just look at how she has overcome and kept moving and it's all because of prayer."

Tee appreciates what he and his mother went through and gives God all the glory for how they both overcame adversity.

"My struggles made me stronger," he added. "God doesn't want me to get down or discouraged. He wants me to keep pushing and keep my head up. Chapel helps me here when I can't get to church on Sunday. This is where I can hear the message and hear God. I love to pray and get my faith stronger."

> *In my distress I called upon the LORD, And cried out to my God; He heard my voice from His temple, And my cry came before Him, even to His ears.*
> —Psalm 18:6 NKJV

4th and Goal

When do you pray? Or do you pray? Do you cry out to the Lord when you are in need? Do you think of Christ as a genie in a bottle? Think of it this way: if you call yourself a Christian, how often or why do you talk to God? Is it important? If you have children, do you want them to communicate with you? How would you feel if your kids only asked for your help in times of trouble. Or how would you feel if they only talked to you once a month. Is prayer a significant part of your life?

Touchdown

For some, prayer is a mere religious ritual. It's only words to be repeated in a congregation. Prayer time might be limited or monitored for approval. But it's much more than going through motions. Prayer can and does change your life if you make time for it. It should never be administered out of obligation. Remember, you get to talk to the Savior. Make time for it every day. Here are benefits of prayer that you cannot do without.

1. Prayer reduces anxiety. When you call upon the Lord and get closer to Him, it makes you calmer and causes you to relax. This is because you turn the focus from your struggles and place your burdens on the Master. When you remove yourself from the cause of stress, you feel better. When you talk to the Lord in prayer and give your problems to Him, you also feel better. "Let the words of my mouth and the meditation of my heart Be acceptable in Your sight, O Lord, my strength and my Redeemer" (Psalm 19:14 NKJV).
2. Prayer invites gratitude. Prayer will bring about a spirit of thankfulness. Start each conversation with God with appreciation for all He's done. Thank Him for the day. Thank Him for life and your health. Thank Him for taking care of you. If you are alive, then thank Him. Thank Him for your blessings and even your troubles. If you have trials and tribulations, those will bring you closer to the Lord. Thank Him. Be grateful.
3. Prayer moves your focus away from you. You could be selfish and the time between you and God could be all

about you, but that would defeat the purpose of prayer. It's OK to pray about your needs, but the Lord already knows your problems and He wants to help and wants you to bring them to Him. But it's also a great time to reflect on others. Ask the Lord to show you ways to help your family or friends. Ask to be used and for wisdom to bring Him honor. "Confess your trespasses to one another, and pray for one another, that you may be healed. The effective, fervent prayer of a righteous man avails much" (James 5:16 NKJV).

4. Prayer can bring about miracles. When you have a real concern and don't know where else to turn, ask for the King of kings to do the miraculous. Take time to fast and place your cares upon Him. Be patient and expect Him to show Himself. The answer may not be the way you want, or it might. In all cases, praise the Lord and give Him glory in advance. "Hear my prayer, O Lord, Give ear to my supplications! In Your faithfulness answer me, And in Your righteousness" (Psalm 143:1 NKJV).

5. Prayer will make you stronger. Cry out in times of temptation and He will provide relief. If you struggle with addiction and are tempted when no one is around, pray and ask for strength. Temptation is not sin. But when you give in to fleshly desires that are wrong, then it becomes sin. Prayer is the best way to fend off worldly distractions and traps set by the devil. The Serenity Prayer is a wonderful prayer, and not just when you are in need. "God, grant me the serenity to accept the things I cannot change, courage

to change the things I can, and the wisdom to know the difference."

In good times and bad, pray. In times of happiness and sadness, pray. You will experience magnificent moments and times of frustration. No matter what—just pray.

Chapter 25

MAKE THE BEST DECISION OF YOUR LIFE

Jordan Kunaszyk
Linebacker

So Jesus said to them, "The light is among you for a little while longer. Walk while you have the light, lest darkness overtake you. The one who walks in the darkness does not know where he is going. While you have the light, believe in the light, that you may become sons of light." When Jesus had said these things, he departed and hid himself from them.
—John 12:35–36

Jordan grew up in Sacramento, California, and was an outstanding athlete. In only his first year of varsity football at Roseville High School, he tallied seventy-seven tackles and three sacks, forced two fumbles, and had two fumble recoveries. Jordan was selected to the second team All Sierra Foothill League and first-team All-Conference.

When he was a senior, he collected 101 tackles (twenty-one for losses) and had one interception and forced a fumble. He was a defensive standout and a wrecking machine for running backs. He knew all about football but little about the Lord and His saving grace.

"I grew up going to church a little bit, but I didn't know a lot about God," he said. "And I didn't have a relationship or know that I could have one. So, when I knew about God's holiness and His righteousness and knew that He would be just in sending me to hell because of my sin . . . and it wasn't until I understood the cross and what that meant . . . that Jesus paid the fine on my behalf so that I could be reconciled with God. It was the greatest decision that I ever made and I'm just so grateful that He led me to that point in my life."

Jordan knew the difference between living like a hypocrite and living with purpose.

"I was living in sin, living in the ways of the world and I was someone who worshipped God with my mouth," he added. "But my lifestyle was not in alignment with Him—and it wasn't until I really understood the reality of where I was going to spend eternity . . . you know, separated from God."

Conviction gripped his heart as hard as he tackled quarterbacks.

"I came to my senses and knew that I am a sinner and in need of a Savior and that God provided a sacrifice in Christ Jesus to free me from my sin and give me the gift of eternal life through repentance and faith," he said. "He convicted my heart and for a long time I could not articulate how the Lord just so dramatically changed me. It took me about a year to realize that this is what it's like to be born again. That moment when God takes your heart of stone and gives you a heart of flesh. Now you have a desire to pursue righteousness when you used to have a desire to pursue sin and things of the world."

The All-Pac 12 Conference and *Sports Illustrated* second-team All-American in college was signed as an undrafted free agent in 2019 by the Carolina Panthers. In 2022, as a member of the Cleveland Browns, he played in fifteen games that included two starts and had a career-high twenty-two tackles. He knows he has a lot of work to do to stay in the NFL, but now he has peace in his heart that only God can give.

"My faith means everything to me, I am a devout follower of the Lord Jesus Christ," he said. "He saved me, and now it's a privilege that I get to be a herald of the gospel message. Not only with my words but with my lifestyle. He saved me three years ago right when I came into the NFL, and I got baptized October 16, 2019."

That is when he said he was living with one foot in religion and one foot out.

"The Lord convicted my heart, and I was born again," he added. "From there, I live my life to honor Him and give Him glory in all that I do."

Therefore put away all filthiness and rampant wickedness and receive with meekness the implanted word, which is able to save your souls.

—James 1:21

4th and Goal

Are you living the way Jordan did with one foot in and one foot out? Maybe you enjoy living like the world during the week and like a pastor on the weekends. Do you know what God has in store for you as a believer? Maybe you might be aware and are running from His calling on your life. Do any of these scenarios describe you? Or maybe you didn't know you can have a personal relationship with Jesus Christ. Are you ready to make the best decision that Jordan made?

Touchdown

If you are tired of living life on the edge or looking for peace of mind, you can find it. It's easy, and the best part is that it doesn't cost you anything material. God paid the price for your salvation when He sent His only Son into the world to die for you and your sins so you can have eternal life. His life for yours. If you are ready to take your relationship with God to the next level, consider these suggestions.

1. See your need for Christ. Without Christ, life is hopeless. It's like the longest two-a-day practice ever. It has no purpose and is grueling. Jesus Christ is the reason you can experience real life and happiness. You can live an abundant and complete life because of Him. "Jesus said to him, 'I am the way, and the truth, and the life. No one comes to the Father except through me'" (John 14:6).
2. Believe the crucifixion and resurrection. Jesus was

placed in a borrowed tomb after His death on the cross. Three days later, He rose from the dead and paid the debt for your sins. He defeated death so you can have life eternal if you accept His sacrifice. "If the Spirit of him who raised Jesus from the dead dwells in you, he who raised Christ Jesus from the dead will also give life to your mortal bodies through his Spirit who dwells in you" (Romans 8:11).

3. Ask Him to forgive you of your sins. Confess your need of Him and the mistakes you have made to Him. Ask Him to cleanse you of your filthiness and give you peace of mind. He will forgive and you can start over. "I acknowledged my sin to you, and I did not cover my iniquity; I said, 'I will confess my transgressions to the LORD,' and you forgave the iniquity of my sin. Selah" (Psalm 32:5).

4. Live a different way. You cannot go back to the ways that had you bound for hell. Once you have experienced His salvation, you need to live your life in a way that is pleasing to God. If this means finding a new crowd to run with, then make the change. No one is worth missing heaven for.

5. Tell others what God did for you. Jordan loves to tell others about how God changed his life. He is happy. He has peace. He has priorities, and he has love for all. Let everyone know the change God made in your life. This will help make you a stronger ambassador for Him. "And he said to them, 'Go into all the world and proclaim the gospel to the whole creation'" (Mark 16:15).

Once you make the commitment, don't hesitate. Forge ahead and enjoy the new journey. Don't go back to your old ways but instead be excited about the promises God has in store for you. This doesn't mean you won't have problems; it means you will have joy in your heart and someone bigger than your issues to help you. Through it all, it will be the best decision you will ever make.

Chapter 26

YOU ARE NEVER "MR. IRRELEVANT" WITH GOD

Brock Purdy
Quarterback

Blessed be the God and Father of our Lord Jesus Christ, who has blessed us in Christ with every spiritual blessing in the heavenly places, even as he chose us in him before the foundation of the world, that we should be holy and blameless before him.
—Ephesians 1:3–4

Since 1936, the final player selected in the NFL Draft has been referred to as "Mr. Irrelevant." The media has made a lot of hype about this nickname, which means the player is of no value or has no meaning. He is irrelevant. Not many expect much from the last player selected and most don't remember his name.

For fans, the NFL Draft is a long and tedious process, and most people don't stick around and listen when the last player is finally picked. Brock earned the nickname in the seventh round of the 2022 NFL Draft when the San Francisco 49ers used the 262nd—and final—selection.

But midway through the season, Brock made a bigger name for himself. Suddenly, he was worth something in the eyes of fans and team owners. He was no longer irrelevant. He was San Francisco's third-string QB but found himself in the starting position on December 11, 2022, after both quarterbacks in front of him went down to injury.

That day he beat Tampa Bay's Tom Brady and became the first rookie to beat the legendary quarterback in his first career start. Brock finished the regular season 5-0 as a starter and was named NFC Rookie of the Month with 1,374 yards passing, thirteen touchdowns, and only four picks.

He was the first "Mr. Irrelevant" signal caller to make it to a divisional playoff round when the 49ers defeated the Dallas Cowboys 19–12. He was also a finalist for NFL Offensive Rookie of the Year (finishing in third place.)

Boy did he prove everyone wrong.

But on January 29, 2022, Brock suffered a complete tear of his ulnar collateral ligament on his throwing arm in a 31–7 loss to the Philadelphia Eagles in the NFL Championship game. Even with that injury, fans and the league knew who Brock was. He was a solid player, who also let everyone know about his faith in Christ.

"You go out there and you prepare to play the best you can," he said. "You get better every single day at practice, and once you get that opportunity, it's what you are going to do with it. For me, I believe in the Lord, and I trust in Him. I just go out there and I just play."

He did not let the fact that he was the last player in the NFL Draft define him as a person or a player. Instead, he allows God to say who he is.

"Every time I play—no matter what happens—I want others to see God through my actions," he said. "Every time I step on the field, I want to bring Him glory. Even when we lose, I point to God and thank Him for the opportunity. Everything happens for a reason, and it's all a lesson from the Lord. It's a game, it's not my life."

Fans buy jerseys with his number and name on the back while others try to snatch an autograph or picture of him. That's part of the territory as an NFL quarterback. But it's not who he is as a person. His identity is in Jesus Christ.

"I continue to lean on Him," he said. "No matter what I'm going to face moving forward, God and Jesus are going to be my identity. And whatever I face, I won't be shaken from it. My foundation is set in Him." That perspective gives his life more meaning than just being a quarterback. He is relevant. He matters to God.

"I don't try to make it more than it is," he added. "I'm a faith-based guy, and that's how I stay grounded. I don't look at football like it's literally everything. It's a game and it's my job and I take that seriously. But at the end of the day, I know that I'm not defined by wins and losses as a person. I'm not just a quarterback and I wasn't born to be a quarterback and play football. I have a life and it matters."

So do you. You matter to God. You are not irrelevant.

For we know, brothers loved by God, that he has chosen you.
—1 Thessalonians 1:4

4th and Goal

Have you ever been made to feel worthless? That you don't matter to anyone. Have circumstances out of your control left you in a mental state of confusion? Words from people can cut deep and leave you feeling like you don't matter. A situation in your life may cause those around you to leave you all alone. If that has happened, then those people may not have loved you with unconditional love. Perhaps your actions brought this on, but you must know there is nothing you've done that God will not forgive. He has plans for you.

Touchdown

Sometimes, you must hit bottom to find your worth. Brock was chosen last in the NFL, but he was indeed selected. No matter the circumstances, one team took him. They may not have expected him to produce the way he did until he was given a chance. While you wait on your opportunity to prove yourself, here are some suggestions on what to do to prepare for that moment.

1. Admit your shortcomings. You cannot and will not be ready to make the first string if you make excuses for your actions. Take a moral inventory of yourself and take note of any scouting report or feedback from others. Improvement will not come if you don't see where you lack. No excuses. Admit when you have wronged someone or yourself and seek forgiveness. "Whoever conceals his transgressions will not prosper, but he who confesses and forsakes them will obtain mercy" (Proverbs 28:13).
2. Seek help. Look to professionals or mentors to help you get back in the game. Find your strength on your knees in prayer and obtain the information you need to assist you in any sort of recovery or self-improvement plan. You matter and keep that in mind. A beautiful pearl is the result of a painful process an oyster endures. "All Scripture is breathed out by God and profitable for teaching, for reproof, for correction, and for training in righteousness" (2 Timothy 3:16).
3. Develop a stubborn determination. Never give up. Possess the attitude that the only people you will ever disappoint are those who expect you to fail. "I have fought the good fight, I have finished the race, I have kept the faith" (2 Timothy 4:7).
4. Set goals. Take these steps at a slow pace and make them realistic. The last thing you want to do is set an expectation so high that it cannot be reached. One day at a time is the best way to reach any goal.
5. Enjoy the wins. When you have a victory, no matter how big or small, celebrate it and move on to the next

round. A win is a win. Notice them and build momentum. Accept small losses or setbacks but celebrate the wins. "Little children, you are from God and have overcome them, for he who is in you is greater than he who is in the world" (1 John 4:4).

Just because someone may have thrown you away does not make you trash. God can and will recycle you and use you for His glory. That makes you relevant in His eyes. Rise to the occasion and blow away low expectations.

Chapter 27

MAKE THE MOST OF YOUR SECOND CHANCE

Damar Hamlin
Safety

This I recall to my mind, therefore have I hope. It is of the LORD's mercies that we are not consumed, because his compassions fail not. They are new every morning: great is thy faithfulness.
—Lamentations 3:21–23 KJV

More than 65,000 people sat in silence and shock during Monday Night Football in Cincinnati on January 2, 2023.

During what appeared to be a routine play, Damar collided with Bengals wide receiver Tee Higgins, fell to the turf, and went into cardiac arrest on the field. Everyone was stunned when Damar's lifeless body fell to the ground early in the second quarter.

Buffalo Bills medical staff rushed onto the field and administered cardiopulmonary resuscitation (CPR) and also used an automated external defibrillator (AED) before they transported Damar to a local hospital.

On the way to the hospital, he flatlined again, but God had other plans. This was evident especially after everyone on the field—both teams included—and thousands seated in the stadium called out to the Lord for help.

The 212th overall pick in the 2021 NFL Draft by the Buffalo Bills survived.

The game was suspended and later canceled the same week. But that was not the main concern. The entire nation was gripped by the story and rejoiced as Damar continued to improve. The University of Pittsburgh product received so much prayer that it suddenly became popular to kneel and pray again on the field.

Believers in Christ knew that God was in control while nonbelievers had to admit that there was more than "luck" to Damar's recovery.

After the Bills defeated New England the week after Damar went down, Buffalo quarterback Josh Allen told the media in a press conference that "I was just going around to my teammates saying, 'God's real.' You can't draw that one up, write that one up any better."

The Bills organization posted a video of Damar on its official Twitter account. In it, Damar addressed his health scare on camera for the first time.

"What happened to me on Monday Night Football, it was a direct example of God using me as a vessel to share my passion and my love directly from my heart with the entire world," he said. "Now, I'm able to give it back to kids and communities all across the world who need it the most and that's always been my dream, that's always been what I stood for and what I will continue to stand for."

After he thanked the trainers and medical staff, teammates, and fans for their support, he went on to give God the glory.

"This is just the beginning of the impact I wanted to have on the world, and with God's guidance, I will continue to do wonderful and great things," he added. "God is using me in a different way today."

God brought Damar back to life because He was not finished with him. And He wanted the entire world to take note of His mighty power. What better way to show His might than on Monday Night Football.

> *Then came Peter to him, and said, Lord, how oft shall my brother sin against me, and I forgive him? till seven times? Jesus saith unto him, I say not unto thee, Until seven times: but, Until seventy times seven.*
>
> —Matthew 18:21–22 KJV

4th and Goal

Life is short. There is no time for bitterness, resentment, and discouragement. The devil wants you to be sidelined with these injuries. He also desires you to die. Satan wants to destroy you and everyone you love. Perhaps your story is not over but is hampered by unforgiveness and hatred. Forgiveness is a wonderful gift, until you are the one who must give it. Do you have unfulfilled goals? Are there people in your life who don't know you love them? Are there people in your life you have distanced yourself from? Do you need a second chance?

Touchdown

God grants forgiveness when you ask. But He won't just give it to you. It must be asked for. The hardest part about this is when you realize you must let go of your sin. Don't ask to take it away because you may still want to hold on to it a little. Give it to Him. Mistakes fester and brew in your mind and memory. Learn from them and move forward. Never return to your old ways but use the pain from the past to motivate you toward success. Here are some suggestions on how to make the most of your second chance.

1. Forgive others. After you have asked God to clean your slate and forgive you of your sins, you should do the same and grant forgiveness. Let go of the feelings the devil planted in your mind from those who may have hurt or offended you. Relationships are important. "But if ye forgive not men their trespasses, neither will your Father forgive your trespasses" (Matthew 6:15 KJV).
2. Be grateful. God gave the life of His only Son so you can live in heaven. Never forget that. He paid the debt of your sin with His blood. "Wherefore we receiving a kingdom which cannot be moved, let us have grace, whereby we may serve God acceptably with reverence and godly fear" (Hebrews 12:28 KJV).
3. Stay focused. Once you have left the past in the locker

room, move forward and be productive for the Lord. Develop a game plan to honor the Lord in moving toward the goal.
4. Get involved. Attend church on a regular basis and be a part of a community and congregation. You matter and have a place. Pay your dues and be ready to play when you are put into the game. Practice and practice by reading your Bible and praying often. Find a ministry to support or volunteer at a local charity. Give back.
5. Praise God always. God is, and has been, good to you. Your day may not go as planned, but as long as you have breath and wake up every day, praise His name for another opportunity. "For the LORD is great, and greatly to be praised: he is to be feared above all gods" (Psalm 96:4 KJV).

God gave Damar a second chance. And Damar said he knows the Lord has plans for him. He has the right attitude. Let's hope you don't have to stare death in the face to realize God has plans for you. But you must be willing to let Him guide you and give you the chance to praise and honor Him.

Chapter 28

DON'T BE SHY ABOUT YOUR FAITH

Patrick Mahomes
Quarterback

Therefore, we are ambassadors for Christ, God making his appeal through us. We implore you on behalf of Christ, be reconciled to God.
—2 Corinthians 5:20

Patrick is a household name to NFL fans, whether they like the team he leads or not. He is a winner and has the hardware to prove it. Patrick has earned countless league awards and at least two Super Bowl rings, two Super Bowl MVP Awards, and two NFL MVP Awards before this book was written. In 2020, he was selected *Sports Illustrated* Sportsman of the Year, and the list of accomplishments goes on and on.

But one title he claims, without hesitation, is being a follower of Jesus Christ. "My Christian faith plays a role in everything I do," he said. "I always ask God to lead me in the right direction."

Patrick is not ashamed to pray before games on the field and does not shy away from his trust in the Lord. "He has a role in everything I do," he added. "I want to make sure I glorify Him while I do it."

Patrick was selected by the Kansas City Chiefs as the tenth pick in the first round of the 2017 NFL Draft. He had an instant impact with Kansas City and, along with head coach Andy Reid, helped turn the team around.

He thrives on giving the Chiefs Kingdom a thrill on the football field but loves to honor the true King of kings.

"Obviously, I want to go out and win every game," he added. "But I'm going to glorify Him every single time I'm out there. As long as I'm doing everything the right way and the way that He would want me to do it, then I can walk off the field with my head held high and be able to be the man that I am."

The 2022 NFL passing yards leader will never back away from a microphone when asked about his salvation.

"I know that I am here for a reason, to glorify Him," he said. "It means everything, not only about my football career but all the decisions that I've made. I have a faith backing, and I know why I am here. It's not about winning football games. It's about glorifying Him."

He not only talked about his faith but added a tattoo based on Acts 20:7–12. In an article in *The Christian Post*, he talked about his skin art.

"It's about being half in and half out on God and the interpretation that I took from it," he said. "You can't be half in and half out. So that was a Bible verse that kind of stuck with me and told me that I need to be fully in."

After the Chiefs knocked off the Cincinnati Bengals 23–20 in the AFC Championship game in 2023, he told Tracy Wolfson of CBS and the entire world about his love for the Master and about how he was healed from an ankle sprain.

"First off, I want to thank God, man," he said on national TV. "He healed my body this week to battle through that. He gave me the strength to be out here."

Patrick knows the importance of giving 100 percent to his craft. He reaps the rewards of hard work and dedication on the field. And he puts the same effort into his relationship with Jesus Christ.

"Without Him, I'd have nothing," he said. "I have my faith, and it's very important to me and my family."

> *And also for me, that words may be given to me in opening my mouth boldly to proclaim the mystery of the gospel.*
> —Ephesians 6:19

4th and Goal

Are you open about your faith? If you had the opportunity to tell the world about your love for Christ, would you? Are you confident in your relationship with Christ to tell millions of people watching on TV about your faith? Now, the chances of you being interviewed on national TV after winning a championship game are slim. But you might be highlighted in your company's newsletter. Or perhaps you get an opportunity to share your faith to a small group of people at work or at a family function. Would you jump at the chance, or let it slide and miss the chance?

Touchdown

Moments like these may not present themselves often. You must be prepared to share your testimony and give God the credit. You want to be careful and not turn off people with what you say. But at the same time, you cannot sugarcoat truths. Tell others about the love of God and His wonderful forgiveness that is free to all who ask for it. Here are some tips on how to be bold enough to share your faith with everyone.

1. Be confident. Patrick did not back down from the microphone after a big win. He thanked God for everyone to hear. To him, it wasn't lip service. He meant what he said. He is confident in his faith because he speaks truth. He knows scripture and puts God first on his priority list. Let others know that the Lord is first in your life and deserves credit for all your blessings. Grow your confidence by reading the word every day and praying. Memorize scripture to help you when moments present themselves.
2. Ask for opportunities. Pray to the Lord for doors to open for you to share your faith. Give thanks for your food in front of others at lunch. This doesn't have to be a long, drawn-out prayer, but the fact that you honor God for the food He provided is a start. Some may

appreciate your stance, and some might find it silly. But most people will respect the gesture. "But in your hearts honor Christ the Lord as holy, always being prepared to make a defense to anyone who asks you for a reason for the hope that is in you; yet do it with gentleness and respect" (1 Peter 3:15).

3. Take to social media. Let your followers know how you feel about Christ. Don't make this your only mission on social media but make it a part of your profile and posts occasionally. Make a post with an inspirational quote with scripture verse. Or just thank the Lord for your blessings after you post a picture of your favorite dessert. Mix it up and have fun and get your point across at the same time. "Blessed be his glorious name forever; may the whole earth be filled with his glory! Amen and Amen!" (Psalm 72:19).

4. Testify in church. Just a simple "thank you, Lord, for all you've done for me" will suffice. A testimony is a way for you to glorify God in public. It's not meant to be a whine session or a time for you to tell everyone how hard your life is. A solid testimony will focus on God's goodness. "Therefore do not be ashamed of the testimony about our Lord, nor of me his prisoner, but share in suffering for the gospel by the power of God" (2 Timothy 1:8).

5. Work it into the conversation. If your friends ask you about your weekend, let them know all about it. But slip in that you went to church and Sunday school and enjoyed the blessings from God. You can tell them you caught three fish or had one birdie on the golf course

or helped your spouse around the house. But slide in bits and pieces about how good God has been to you.

You may never stand at the fifty-yard line and celebrate a Super Bowl win, but you do have your chances to talk about the Lord. Don't back down or be ashamed. Be bold and let everyone know about your faith.

Chapter 29

BE WHO GOD MADE YOU TO BE

Jalen Hurts
Quarterback

For you formed my inward parts; you knitted me together in my mother's womb. I praise you, for I am fearfully and wonderfully made. Wonderful are your works; my soul knows it very well. My frame was not hidden from you, when I was being made in secret, intricately woven in the depths of the earth. Your eyes saw my unformed substance; in your book were written, every one of them, the days that were formed for me, when as yet there was none of them.
—Psalm 139:13–16

Professional football players are put on a pedestal by some fans. A lot of younger athletes might pretend to be Jalen Hurts on the football field. And why not? Jalen is a remarkable quarterback whom God has blessed with tremendous ability.

It's OK to admire a player for their accomplishments or their work ethic. But some fans get caught up in the hype and try to actually play with a similar style. You might try to throw or run like Jalen on the field. Although that might be admirable, it can also be a detriment.

God made Jalen to be Jalen. And He made you to be you. And to be honest, there is only one Jalen Hurts. The fifty-third overall pick in the 2020 NFL Draft from Oklahoma makes his presence known on the football field without a doubt.

Defensive coordinators stay up at night and try to find ways to stop Jalen, but they haven't found a way yet to slow down the Pro Bowl QB. When this book was written, Jalen was a fan favorite in the City of Brotherly Love.

In 2022, he played like a seasoned veteran and led the Eagles to Super Bowl LVII. But even with the early success in the NFL, Jalen is aware that he is led by a Higher Power.

"I've just matured and realized that God is everything," Hurts said in an interview with CBS Sports. "And He's worthy of praise. You have to put Him at the center of everything that you do. That's what I believe. All my spiritual wisdom—all of my wisdom as a whole—comes from Him, in some way, shape, or form, whether that be passed down from my father, my mother, my grandmother. I just think, in all the things that we experience in life—good, bad, or indifferent—you have to keep Him in the center."

Jalen relied on his faith, especially when he decided to transfer from Alabama to Oklahoma for his senior year of college. He is also aware of his worth as a Christian athlete and does not take for granted the blessings and opportunities that have come from the Lord. Jalen knows that he is unique and wants to be who Christ wants him to be.

"God only made me one way," he said in the interview with CBS Sports. "That's to be me. That's to be Jalen Hurts. I think, being in this city, being the quarterback for the Philadelphia Eagles, and just having the opportunity to play the game I love most, in the best city of football, I just go out there every day and I am who I am, and I keep God in the center, I give Him all the praise, I lean on Him all the time, and I know that everything unfolds the way it's supposed to."

> *Now the word of the LORD came to me, saying, "Before I formed you in the womb I knew you, and before you were born I consecrated you; I appointed you a prophet to the nations."*
> —Jeremiah 1:4–5

4th and Goal

Who are you? Do you try to act like someone you might look up to? Do you find yourself impersonating someone you like? Do you lack self-confidence? Maybe you grew up in the shadow of a sibling or feel you never lived up to expectations. Maybe many circumstances have caused you to doubt your own ability or calling in life.

Touchdown

In Psalm 139, David expresses that he is fearfully and wonderfully made. And so are you. If the Lord can use David, then He can use you too. You matter and have a dynamic purpose. But you must be who God made you to be. You will not move forward if you act like someone else. King David committed adultery and had his lover's husband killed in battle. He also suffered from emotional issues and was discouraged in his walk. But God had different plans for David. And God has plans for you too. Here are some tips to consider your worth as a child of the King.

1. Repent. If you have done something wrong that is not in the will of the Lord, seek and ask for forgiveness of sin. You might get away with doing wrong for a season, but you will never be used by God until you seek His forgiveness. You will reap what you sow. Make sure your heart is good with the Lord and that you have peace that only God can grant. This is the first step in realizing your true calling from the Lord. "Repent therefore, and turn back, that your sins may be blotted out" (Acts 3:19).
2. Use your talents. Everyone has ability and talent. Seek God's face and His will in your life. Not everyone can sing (although some who can't think they can). Not everyone is called to be a preacher. You don't have to be in the limelight. Maybe you have the gift of art or writing. Perhaps your talent is visiting or baking pies or sending out cards. Your talent might be in construction or in teaching. If you enjoy a hobby, then consider that to be your talent. Whatever talent you have, use it to glorify the Master.
3. Be patient. Don't do something because *you* think it's the best move. If something doesn't transpire, then it might not be meant to be. If you have to force an issue, then maybe you are the one in the way. If you are not

sure of your talent, then sit back, read your Bible, and pray as long as it takes. For some, God might reveal their talents early. But if this has not happened, you might have to wait on His timing. "But if we hope for what we do not see, we wait for it with patience" (Romans 8:25).

4. Be bold. Step out in faith and be happy that God has plans for you. Whatever He wants you to do, then do it with all that is inside you. You are a child of God and wear that banner with pride, although you never let that show to others. Let everyone see a humble heart that is being inspired by Christ. "The wicked flee when no one pursues, but the righteous are bold as a lion" (Proverbs 28:1).

5. Don't listen to naysayers. The devil likes to discourage. He also loves to use people to do his dirty work. If someone complains or makes fun of your efforts to praise the Lord through your talents, don't listen to them. "The name of the LORD is a strong tower; the righteous man runs into it and is safe" (Proverbs 18:10).

Jalen plays like Jalen. He knows and is confident in his talent and ability. You should be the same way. If you have a talent for math, then use it to bring honor to the heavenly Father. If your talent is organization, then find a ministry and get involved. God made you to be you and no one else. Use others like King David or Jalen as inspiration but never as imitation. Be you.

Chapter 30

KNOW YOUR PURPOSE

Cooper Kupp
Wide Receiver

For still the vision awaits its appointed time; it hastens to the end—it will not lie. If it seems slow, wait for it; it will surely come; it will not delay.

—Habakkuk 2:3

Super Bowl rings must be great to wear and display. Will you ever win one? Odds are the answer is no. But you may know someone who knows someone who has one.

A close friend of mine is an MLB scout, and when his team won the World Series, he received his bling ring special delivery. He did not waste time wearing it to a local high school football game.

It was impressive.

The humongous ring was a reward for a job well done. It signified and represented greatness.

Another close friend was a major part of the Pittsburgh Pirates World Series Championship in 1971. Even back then, those rings were enormous. Al wears it everywhere he goes. And why not?

Cooper earned the NFL's biggest reward when he helped the Los Angeles Rams win Super Bowl LVI over the Cincinnati Bengals. The Eastern Washington University product not only took home the Vince Lombardi Trophy but was also named the Super Bowl MVP.

Cooper enjoyed a banner 2021 season. In addition to the Super Bowl and game-MVP award, he was named the NFL Offensive Player of the Year, chosen First Team All-Pro, selected to the Pro Bowl, and led the league in catches, yards, and most receiving touchdowns. He did it all. He admitted that he liked the recognition but added that all the glory goes to the Lord.

"My motivation coming in every single day is to run the race in such a way as to honor God and the passions and the talents that He's given me," he told the media. "When I am rooted in that, I'm in a great place. I am able to play freely."

But even with all the accolades, Cooper knows his purpose in life. "I think the thing that [God] has taught me is that you will find that you are most fulfilled, you will find the most joy, when you are rooted in your purpose, and specifically rooted in His purpose for you," he told the media before the Super Bowl. "And that, to me, has been one of the best things about this year."

A young kid reporter posed a question to Cooper and asked him what motivates him to be the best version of himself.

"Because I knew that football is something God had given to me to pursue," he answered. "My drive wasn't to achieve for myself in any regard. There weren't goals or anything I wanted to achieve or any honors that I was striving for. I was really about each day being able to wake up and say, 'I want to be the best that I can possibly be for no other reason than that God has put me here and I want to honor that and respect that to the best of my ability.'

"Now I get to come into work with the greatest purpose, with the greatest drive, the greatest goals in mind because that is the perspective I get to take. That's really what drives me in everything I do, whether it's being the best football player I can be, being the best man I can be, being the best son, the best husband, the best father."

After the Rams won the Super Bowl, Cooper told the same media he spoke to before the game the same message. Nothing changed.

"I got to a place where I was validated not from anything that happened on the field because of my worth in God and in my Father," he said. "And I'm just so incredibly thankful."

A ring and Super Bowl trophy did not redirect his perspective for his purpose with the Lord.

> *Declaring the end from the beginning and from ancient times things not yet done, saying, "My counsel shall stand, and I will accomplish all my purpose."*
> —Isaiah 46:10

4th and Goal

Do you know what God wants for your life? If you know, then congratulations and keep focused on His plan. But if you do not know, then you probably have a lot of questions. There are conflicting opinions on this, especially if you ask your friends or pastors about God's plan. Some might tell you that you must seek after the Lord for His specific plan for your life. Others may tell you that everything you do is part of the plan. How are you to know? Why would you go to college for four years only to take a job that doesn't require a degree? Or why are there no careers in the area that interest you? Or why are you in a specific part of the country that you may not even like? What does God want for your life? Why did the person you love break up with you? Why are you spinning in circles?

Touchdown

There is one clear answer to all questions. The Lord wants you to bring honor and glory to His name no matter what you do or where you are. But although there is one answer from Christ, you still may have several questions that rattle around in the back of your mind. What does God want me to do? How does He want me to do it? When will He reveal to me His plan? Will I be able to support myself? What will others think? Questions and more questions. But while you pray and seek God's direction for your life, ponder these questions to yourself.

1. What talents has God given to you? You have a purpose and a talent. In Cooper's case, he can catch a football like nobody's business. Can you sing for the Lord? Is your talent drawing? Maybe writing? Perhaps your talent is visiting people or showing support or praying for others. God will not have you do something that He

has not equipped you for. Use your gifts for His glory.
2. What do you enjoy doing? Working for the Lord does not mean you will be employed by a ministry. But it might. Find a job or allow the Lord to direct you to an occupation you like to do. Keep in mind this is something you may spend thirty years doing, so be sure to like the journey. Can you be redirected? Yes. But never get in His way. God will direct your path as long as you are in His will for your life. Ask Him to open the doors for you to walk through. Philippians 4:6 encourages you to "let your requests be made known to God."
3. How can you make a positive impact? You can do this in several easy ways. You can smile and be kind to others. You can find an interest in local politics or other civic organizations to make a difference. Run for school board or join a group that does good deeds in the area. "Whatever you do, work heartily, as for the Lord and not for men" (Colossians 3:23).
4. How can you help others? Develop a generous heart. Give and help those who are hurting. Volunteer your time or teach Sunday school or lead a small group. Give back with sincere intent and never expect a reward in return. "Blessed is the one who considers the poor! In the day of trouble the LORD delivers him" (Psalm 41:1).
5. Will this bring glory to Him? In all you do, give Him honor. You may not like your current job, but praise His name for the one you have at the moment. How will God bless you with a better job if you are not thankful for the one you have? Apply that scenario in other areas of life. "My lips will shout for joy, when

I sing praises to you; my soul also, which you have redeemed" (Psalm 71:23).

Cooper was asked a lot of questions before and after the Super Bowl. In all ways, he praised the Lord and thanked Him for His goodness. You have a purpose and gifts from the Lord. Praise Him today and He will bless you tomorrow. God is good—all the time.

Milton Keynes UK
Ingram Content Group UK Ltd.
UKHW051340140724
445326UK00014BA/575